Guess Wh

-Intercultural Surprises-

Comprehensive Training for English "5" Skills:

Read, Listen, Write, Speak, and Discuss!

世界の衝撃アイテムから学ぶ
15の国の文化と人々

読んで聞いて書いて話して議論する！
英語「5」技能総合訓練教材

by

Natsuki Matsui

Yasuhiro Iida

Naoko Kaneda

Ken Wing Poon

≪ Adviser ≫

Hitoshi Yokoyama

NAN'UN-DO

Guess What?!

- Intercultural Surprises -

Comprehensive Training for English "5" Skills:

Read, Listen, Write, Speak, and Discuss!

by

Natsuki Matsui / Yasuhiro Iida

Naoko Kaneda / Ken Wing Poon

Hitoshi Yokoyama (Adviser)

Download Audio

音声ファイル
無料 DL
のご案内

このテキストの音声を無料で視聴（ストリーミング）・ダウンロードできます。自習用音声としてご活用ください。
以下のサイトにアクセスしてテキスト番号で検索してください。

https://nanun-do.com　テキスト番号［**512113**］

※ 無線 LAN（WiFi）に接続してのご利用を推奨いたします。

※ 音声ダウンロードは Zip ファイルでの提供になります。
お使いの機器によっては別途ソフトウェア（アプリケーション）の導入が必要となります。

Read by

Karen Haedrich（アメリカ英語）
Chris Koprowski（アメリカ英語）
Ian Bell　（オーストラリア英語）

※ Guess What?! の音声ダウンロードページは以下の QR コードからもご利用になれます。

はじめに

近年、グローバル化が急速に進み、国際交流を意識する機会が増えました。インターネットやソーシャルメディアも普及し、世界の国々の人口や公用語などはもちろん、その国の文化や国民性などについても容易に知ることが可能になり、まるでその国に行ったかのような気分にさせてくれるサイトもあります。基本的には本書でも、15 ユニットの学習を通して英語力の向上を目指しつつ、15 の国への「バーチャル世界旅行」を楽しんでもらいます。

ここまではよくありそうな英語テキストの内容ですが、本書のユニークな点は、世界の国々に存在する衝撃アイテムに注目しているところです。「日本ではそんな物は絶対に売れない！」、「日本ではそんな使い方は絶対にしない！」というような、我々の目には奇異に映るアイテムを取り上げ、各ユニットで“Guess what?!”（何だと思う？！）と問いかけながら紹介します。そして、そのアイテムがなぜその国で愛され、長年使用されているのかを知ることから、異文化理解を深めるようにできているのです。

本書が揃えた世界の衝撃アイテムは、日用品や家電製品や乗り物、またスポーツ応援グッズなど、バラエティに富んでおり、これらを通して世界各国の文化・風習・歴史・気候・宗教・人種・食文化・交通事情など、興味深い側面を多角的に英語で学んでもらいます。初級～中級レベルの英語学習者に広く対応できる中身になっており、各ユニットの学習を通して、異文化理解と総合的な英語力のアップを同時に達成できる構成になっています。

本書の特徴

1. どのユニットから学んでも大丈夫な、異文化理解に役立つ 400 語程度の英文エッセイ
2. TOEIC® L&R 対策問題を含んだ、4 技能向上のための豊富なエクササイズ
3. 15 の国を深く知るために役に立つ、多種多様な写真
4. 15 の国の食文化の知識を深め、口語表現も学べる会話問題
5. 15 の国の言語を知り、文化的ミニ知識が増えるコラム
6. 仲間との意見交換でディスカッション能力を伸ばす、ディクトグロス風アクティビティ

最後に、本書の制作にあたっては著者陣の友人や同僚など、現地の方々や現地をよく知る世界中の方々に情報提供や原稿チェックのご協力をいただきました。また南雲堂の田中仁氏、丸小雅臣氏（現・開文社社長）には、企画の当初から長期間にわたって多くのご助言や励ましをいただきました。ここに感謝を申し上げます。

2020 年　夏

著者一同

本書の使い方

■　本書の構成

各章 6 ページで、15 章で構成されています。

■　各章の構成

Pre-Reading Activity

各 Unit のテーマである国の衝撃アイテムなどの数枚の写真があります。ここでは正解のないクイズを出していますので、自由な発想でクラスメートと英語で思いついたことを話しましょう。

Vocabulary Map

Reading の重要語彙が散りばめられています。関連性を考えて選択肢から語を選びましょう。

Reading

各 Unit のテーマである国の衝撃アイテムと文化的背景が紹介されています。重要語彙がまとめてある Words and Phrases の空所を埋めてから、本文を読み、その国の文化や国民性の一面を学びましょう。また、ここでは Pre-Reading Activity の写真についての詳細も知ることができます。

Reading Exercises

Reading の内容に関する問題です。各設問に答えて文法力・読解力を強化しましょう

A TOEIC® L&R の Part 2 形式の問題です。音声を聞き、本文の内容と合致するものを選びましょう。問題が進むにつれて印刷されている部分は減っていきます。

B TOEIC® L&R の Part 5 形式の問題です。空所に入る最も適切な語句を選びます。

C Reading の内容に関して、記述が正しいか誤っているかを判断します。

D Reading 内の重要表現を、語句を並べ替えてライティングすることで記憶させます。

Conversation

日本人とその国出身の留学生との会話から、Unit のテーマである国の食文化について学びます。会話を聞きながら解答する問題と、会話を聞いてから写真を見て解答する問題があります。解答後は 3 人でロールプレイをするとスピーキング力の向上にもなります。

Column

各 Unit で取り上げられている国の言語と文化についてのコラムです。その国特有の興味深い表現や格言などが紹介されており、言語表現から異文化理解を深めます。

Group Presentation

1) Reading の内容に関わる 2 種類の意見文から片方を選び、その理由を書きます。
2) 同意見の人とグループを作り、英語で自分の考えを述べます。他の人が話しているとき、キーワードとなる英単語をメモしましょう。
3) 全員がメモしたキーワードを基に、グループとしての意見をまとめた英文を作りましょう。（ディクトグロスを想定した練習）
4) クラスで各グループがプレゼンテーションをし、他グループの意見についても議論しましょう。

Table of Contents

The Map of Our Journey

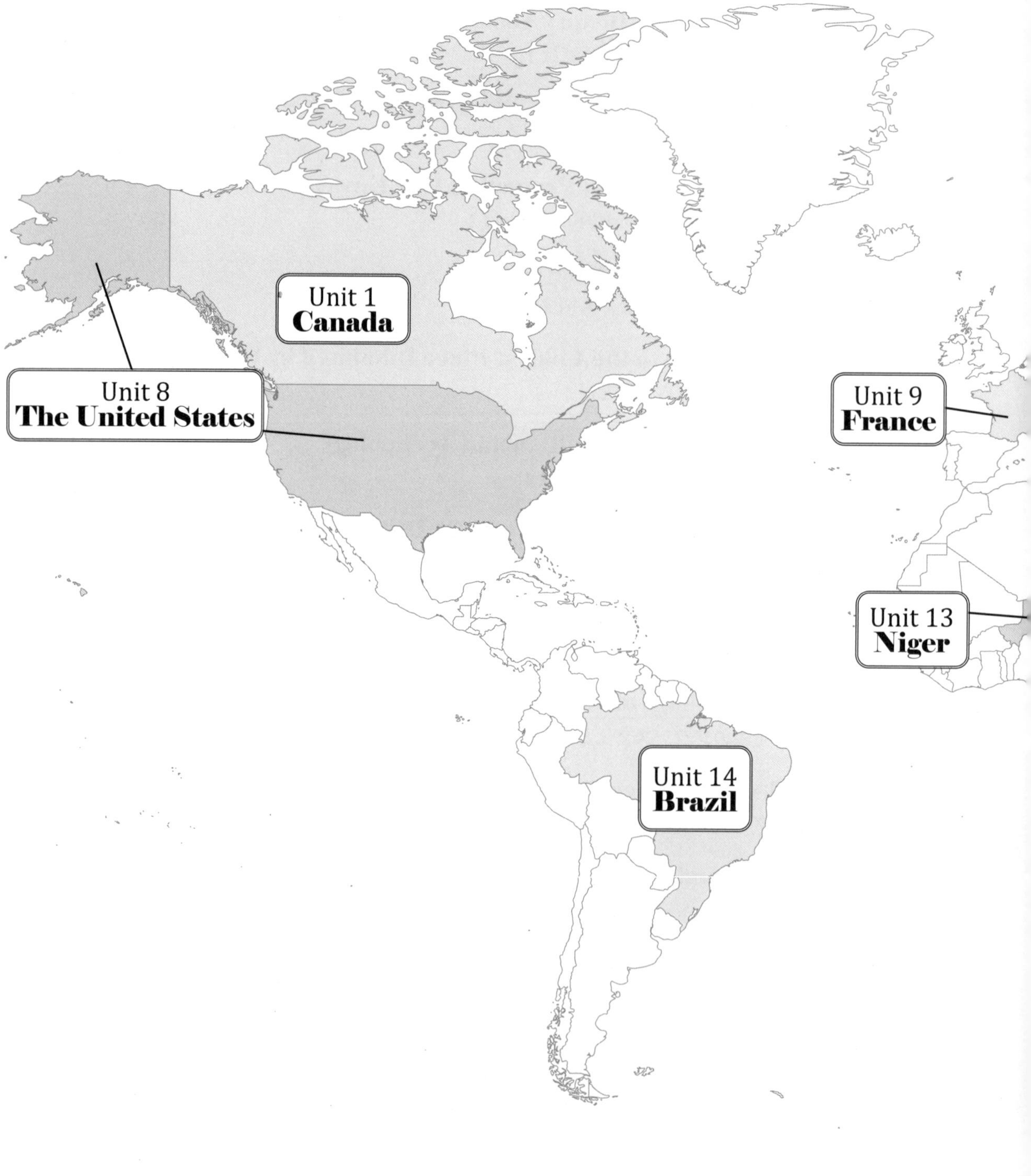

nit 15
weden
Unit 5
Russia
Unit 3
Germany
Unit 4
Turkey
Unit 10
Bangladesh
Unit 12
South Korea
Unit 6
Israel
Unit 2
Thailand
Unit 7
South Africa
Unit 11
New Zealand

Unit 1

Canada: Natural Beauty Abounds

自然に恵まれた調和の文化とは！

Pre-Reading Activity

Look at picture 1. Guess what the buckets are for. Talk to your partner in English.

Vocabulary Map

Use the words in the box to complete the vocabulary map.

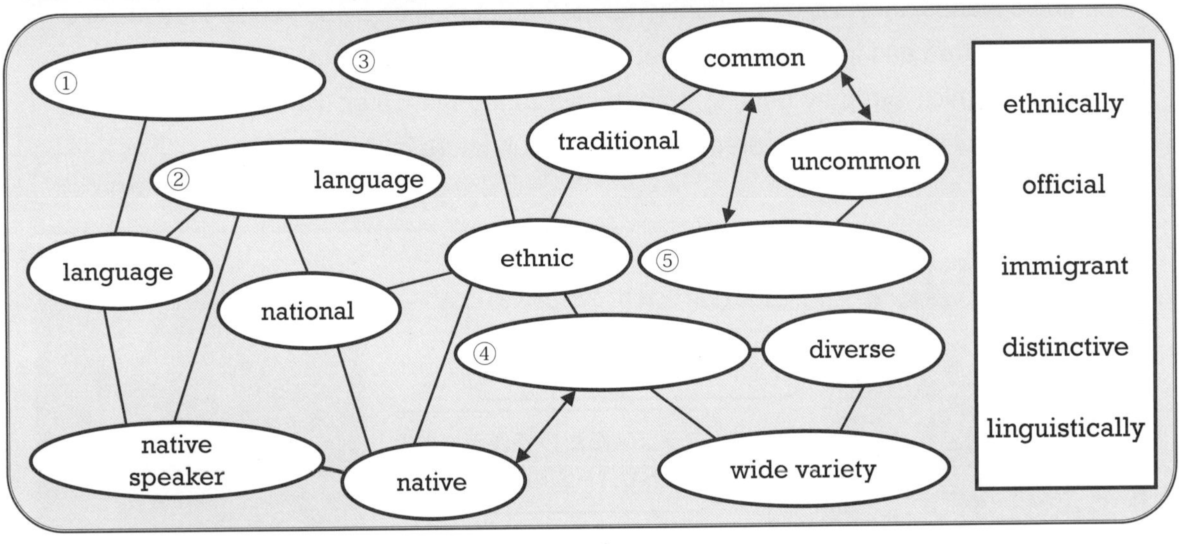

Reading

Canada is a country blessed with nature. Every year, tourists are amazed by the impressive sights such as the Rocky Mountains and Niagara Falls. The seasons also bring brilliantly colored leaves in the fall, and a snowy wonderland in the winter. Therefore, it is no wonder that Canadians are proud of their natural wonders.

Canada has a long winter, so people take advantage of it. Winter sports on ice are very popular, and there are a lot of inside and outside ice-skating rinks. Although some might think Canadians are calm and polite, they may behave like a whole different person when it comes to their national sport, ice hockey. Many Canadians often shout out to cheer for their home team with their friends or family when the game is on.

Canada and America are geographically in North America, and they speak in the same North American accent. Some people think these two countries are similar, but Canada has its own distinctive culture. You might see tourists around the world who have a Canadian flag badge or emblem on their bag. These items are there to say, "I'm Canadian not American." This is their way of calmly expressing pride in their country.

In Canada, not everyone is a native speaker of English; there are a wide variety of languages spoken. It is ethnically and linguistically diverse, so English is not always the main language in some provinces. The country is composed of native Canadians and other immigrants from all over the world. As a result, both English and French are official languages, and so you might see many things like road signs and food packages written in both languages. In fact, in the province called Quebec, which is in eastern Canada, French is the official language, and they have a different culture established there.

One of Canada's most famous exports is maple syrup, and most of it comes from Quebec. The natural syrup is extracted from trees called "sugar maple." Did you know, in some places, they still use a traditional method of making syrup? First, they make a hole in the tree and insert a tap so that the sap runs into a bucket. Then, they turn the sap into a thick syrup by heating it and evaporating the water. Through enjoying this sweet syrup, we can also appreciate the beautiful nature in Canada.

(394 words)

「止まれ」を表すフランス語だけで表示されたケベック州モントリオールの道路標識

フランス語だけで表示されたモントリオールのスクールバス

Find the following words in a dictionary and write their meanings in the parentheses below. Fill in the bracket with an appropriate word to complete the phrase.

Words and Phrases ★ 予習しておこう！

be blessed with ~	～に恵まれている	linguistically	言語的に
be amazed by ~	～に驚かされる	diverse	(　　　　　　　)
impressive	印象的な、すばらしい	be composed of ~	～で構成される
no wonder	不思議ではない	immigrant	移民
natural wonder	自然のすばらしさ	official language	公用語
take advantage of ~	～をうまく利用する	road sign	道路標識
calm	(　　　　　　　)	province	（カナダなどの）州
whole different	まったく異なる	established	確立した
when it comes [　　] ~	～のことになると	exports	(　　　　　　　)
shout out	大声を出す	be extracted from ~	～から抽出される
geographically	地理的に	insert	さし込む
accent	なまり	tap	蛇口、栓
distinctive	(　　　　　　　)	turn … into ~	…を～に変える
a wide variety of ~	さまざまな～	evaporate	蒸発させる
ethnically	(　　　　　　　)	appreciate	よさを認める

Reading Exercises

A *You will hear three questions about the passage. Select the best answer and circle (A), (B) or (C).* 3

1. When are Canadians most likely to get excited?
   (A) When they watch ice hockey games on TV.
   (B) When they visit Niagara Falls for sightseeing.
   (C) When they eat food with famous maple syrup.

2.
   (A) A lot of
   (B) Many
   (C) Most of

3.
   (A)
   (B)
   (C)

B *Circle the best choice to complete the following sentences.*

1. Canada has a long winter, so people _____ advantage of it.

(A) force
(B) launch
(C) propose
(D) take

2. These items are _____, "I'm Canadian not American."

(A) there to say
(B) there are say
(C) to there say
(D) say there to

3. Canada is ethnically and linguistically _____, so English is not always the main language in some provinces.

(A) differ
(B) difference
(C) diverse
(D) diversity

4. They still use a traditional _____ of making syrup.

(A) hands
(B) method
(C) suffering
(D) tongue

C *Based on the information in the passage, write "T" if it is true, or "F" if it is false.*

1. Canada and the U.S. are located on the same continent. ( )
2. English and French are the only languages spoken in Canada. ( )
3. The sugar maple is one of Canada's most famous exports. ( )

D *Rearrange the words and phrases in the ( ) to complete the sentences.*

1. カナダ人が自分たちの自然のすばらしさを誇りに思うことは不思議ではない。
It (Canadians / no / is / are / proud / that / wonder) of their natural wonders.
It (______________________________
______________________________) of their natural wonders.

2. 木に穴を開け、蛇口をさし込むことで樹液がバケツへと流れこむのである。
They make a hole in the tree and (so / runs / a tap / the sap / insert / into / that) a bucket.
They make a hole in the tree and (______________________________
______________________________) a bucket.

Conversation

Listen to the conversation and answer the following. For ①, put the words in the { } in the right order. For ② and ③, fill in the blanks. For ④, choose the right words.

Kenta: Yesterday, I watched a movie set in Canada, and I saw a scene where an American character was disappointed to find mayonnaise on his burger.

Matt: It ① ({ like / it / place / sounds / took }→ ______________________________ ______________________________) in Quebec. It's different from the other regions of Canada. Most of the people there are French Canadians.

Jeanne: Our culture is influenced by the French, who love mayonnaise, so...

Matt: Yeah, I heard Quebecois even eat french fries with mayonnaise, which isn't common in Vancouver. ② (______________________) , I like ketchup and mustard.

Kenta: Oh, wow. You Canadians are quite different depending on where you're from. Even the way you eat french fries isn't the same!

Jeanne: But we have this dish called "poutine." I guess it's common throughout Canada.

Kenta: Poutine? I've never heard of that. What's ③ (______________) (______________) ?

Matt: It's made with fries and cheese curds, with gravy on top. You can have it at fast food restaurants in Canada.

Kenta: What is gravy?

Jeanne: Gravy is a thick sauce made from the juices of meats. We usually ④ { put it on / pull it up / pot it out } meat dishes. However, for real poutine, we put "brown sauce" on it.

Choose the picture that does not match the conversation and circle the number.

(1)

(2)

(3)

(4)

Column

文化を知るための Language：英語・フランス語 (English/Français)

***eh*「エイ」／*Bienvenue*「ビアンヴニュ」**

カナダ人の英語を聞いてもカナダ人なのかアメリカ人なのかは発音だけでは聞き分けがなかなかできません。しかし、カナダ人英語として必ず話題になる表現はあります。「〜だよね？」というときに使う *eh?* です。アメリカだと〜, *right?*（〜でしょ？）と言うところが、カナダだと〜, *eh?* となります。この *eh?* が出てくると、実にカナダ人英語らしくなるそうです。

一方、カナダ人のフランス語は、フランス人のフランス語とかなり違います。発音ですぐにカナダ人だとわかります。カナダのフランス語にはフランス革命時代の発音が残っているそうです。また、話しことばでは、語彙や文法もフランスのものと少し違います。たとえば、*Bienvenue* は「ようこそ」という意味ですが、カナダでは「ようこそ」だけでなく、「どういたしまして」という意味でも使われています。カナダのフランス語は *Québécois*（ケベコワ）と呼ばれ、英語からの借用語も多く、フランスのフランス語とは異なる言語の進化を遂げているようです。

Group Presentation

1. Which do you prefer, (A) or (B)? Put a check mark (✓) and write your reason in the box.

☐ (A) I prefer to spend my life living in a place surrounded by nature.

☐ (B) I prefer to spend my life living in an urban city.

Because ……………………………………………………………………

2. Make a group with two or three partners who have the same preference and present your thoughts. Write down the important key words in each box while listening to others.

Key words: Group member 1	Key words: Group member 2	Key words: Group member 3

3. Using your group member's key words, form one collective opinion.

4. Present your group's opinion to the class.

Unit 2

Thailand: Where Culture and Fragrance Harmonize

香りにこだわる文化とは！

Pre-Reading Activity

Look at picture 2. Guess what the person is doing. Talk to your partner in English.

1

2
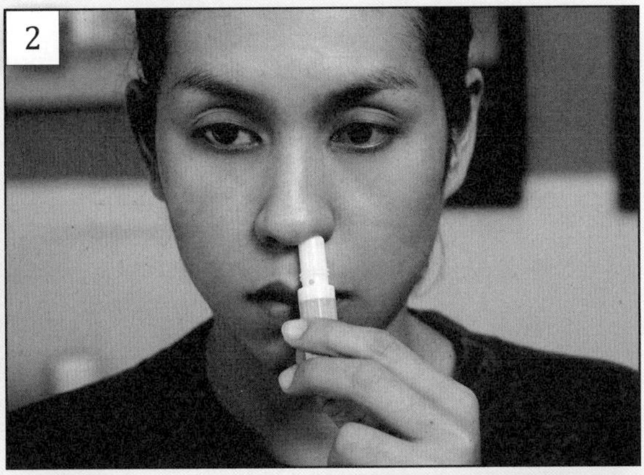

3

4

5

6
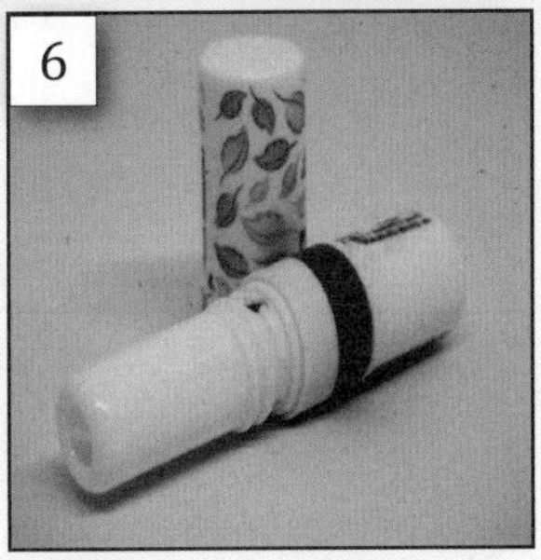

Vocabulary Map

Use the words in the box to complete the vocabulary map.

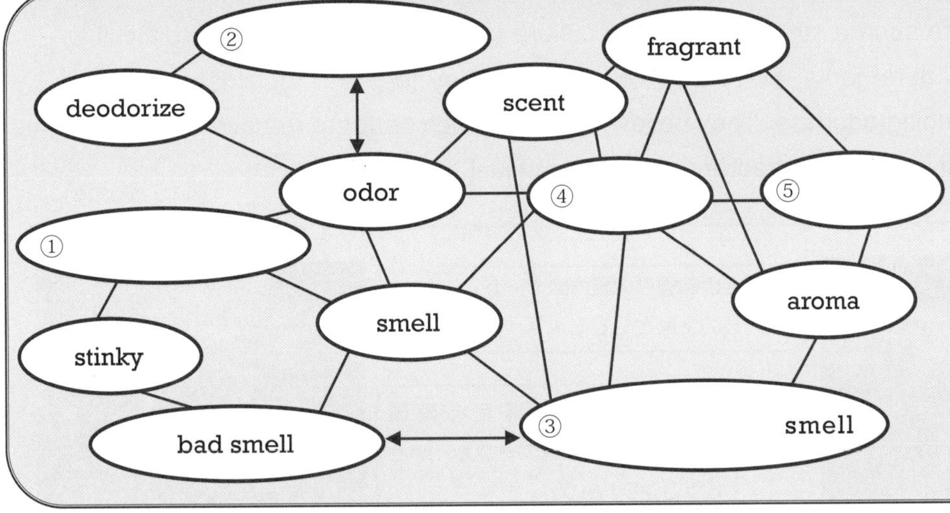

odorless

fragrance

pleasant

smelly

aromatic

Reading

5

Smells and fragrances play a big part in the culture and lifestyle in Thailand. While Japanese people try to remain as odorless as possible, the Thai people enjoy different aromas using products with pleasant smells.

One of the products is called *yadom*. In Thailand, you may frequently notice people placing a small plastic tube into their noses and inhaling. This item that looks like a glue stick is *yadom*. It is an inhaler that is often filled with essential oils from natural ingredients. It is used to energize and relieve nasal congestion and is available across the country in convenience stores, supermarkets, drugstores, and general stores in Thailand. It is not uncommon to see someone using a *yadom* out in public, in the classroom, in restaurants, or anywhere else! Many visitors to Thailand are quite surprised to see the wide use of *yadom*. You may even see groups of young girls casually placing the *yadom* into their noses and inhaling.

It is said that the scents of *yadom* can help to improve your mood and fight off drowsiness as well. Thai students often use *yadom* to help them concentrate on their studies. In fact, many university students say that they need to have their *yadom* with them, especially when they take an exam! During an exam, Thai students are not allowed to have anything else on them except for their student ID card and a pen. But despite this, a common question that the students ask is, “May I bring my *yadom* with me to my seat?”

For the Thai people, fragrance is an important part of their lives. They often use the word *horm*, which means “fragrant, aromatic, and pleasant-smelling.” They strongly prefer products that can be described as *horm*. That means products such as laundry detergents, soaps, and lip balms should all have a pleasing scent. The scents themselves are also unique, like the scent of tropical fruits and plants found in Thailand.

Compared to Thai people, the Japanese do not seem to place as much importance on strong fragrances. Japanese people are often fond of subtle aromas. However, fragrances are such a strong part of the culture in Thailand that it is very difficult to find odorless detergents. For many Thai people, they feel that there is no point in making something odorless. They believe that it is much better to remove a bad smell by replacing it with a good fragrance, rather than just deodorizing it.

(410 words)

さまざまな香りの種類のヤードム。観光客の土産としても人気

市場や屋台でも買える南国フルーツ。写真はスターフルーツとドラゴンフルーツ

Find the following words in a dictionary and write their meanings in the parentheses below. Fill in the bracket with an appropriate word to complete the phrase.

Words and Phrases ★予習しておこう！

fragrance	(　　　　　　)	scent	(　　　　　　)
play a big part	大きな役割を果たす	improve one's mood	気分をよくする
remain	～のままである	fight off drowsiness	眠気と戦う
odorless	(　　　　　　)	concentrate on ~	～に集中する
aroma	（心地よい）香り、匂い	be allowed to ~	～ことが許される
pleasant	気持ちよい、心地よい	despite ~	～にもかかわらず
inhale	吸い込む	fragrant	(　　　　　　)
glue stick	スティックのり	aromatic	芳香の
ingredient	材料、原料	laundry detergent	洗濯洗剤
energize	元気づける、活発にする	unique	独特の、特有の
relieve	和らげる、軽減する	compared to ~	～と比べると
nasal congestion	鼻づまり	be fond of ~	～が好き
be available	入手できる	subtle	ほのかな、かすかな
general store	（日用品の）雑貨屋	remove	取り除く
out in public	公の場で、人前で	replace A [　　　] B	B と A を取り替える
casually	何気なく	deodorize	(　　　　　　)

Reading Exercises

A *You will hear three questions about the passage. Select the best answer and circle (A), (B) or (C).* 6

1. What may surprise visitors to Thailand?
   (A) Odorless detergents available in plants
   (B) University students excited about exams
   (C) People putting small tubes in their noses

2.
   (A) Have
   (B) Play
   (C) Smell

3.
   (A)
   (B)
   (C)

B *Circle the best choice to complete the following sentences.*

1. You may frequently notice people placing a small plastic tube into their noses and _____.

(A) inhale
(B) inhaled
(C) inhaling
(D) to inhale

2. It is used to _____ and relieve nasal congestion.

(A) energy
(B) energize
(C) energetic
(D) enervate

3. Thai students often use *yadom* to help them _____ their studies.

(A) concentrate on
(B) take part in
(C) look after
(D) turn down

4. That means products _____ as laundry detergents should have a pleasing scent.

(A) that
(B) many
(C) due
(D) such

C *Based on the information in the passage, write "T" if it is true, or "F" if it is false.*

1. Strong fragrances play a more important role in Thailand than Japan. (   )
2. *Yadom* helps people in Thailand to be more physically developed. (   )
3. In Thailand, people keep tropical fruits at home to clean their clothes. (   )

D *Rearrange the words and phrases in the (   ) to complete the sentences.*

1. タイの人々は無臭の商品を作ることに意味はないと感じている。

Thai people think that (point / is / there / making / in / odorless / no) products.

Thai people think that (____

____) products.

2. 嫌な臭いはいい匂いと取り替えたほうがよい。

It is (replace / better / to / smell / with / bad / a) a good fragrance.

It is (____

______________________________) a good fragrance.

Conversation

Listen to the conversation and answer the following. For ①, choose the right words. For ② and ④, fill in the blanks. For ③, put the words in the { } in the right order. 7

Kenta: How was the new Thai restaurant near the university?

Bean: Well, it was quite authentic but a bit too expensive for me.

Kenta: Speaking ① { off which / of which / of itch }, is it possible to eat good Thai food at food stalls in Thailand?

Huat: Yes, but lately food stalls are disappearing in Bangkok.

Bean: Street food has been ② (   ) by the government, so you see fewer food stalls than before.

Kenta: Really? Does it mean you will have no street food in the near future?

Bean: No, I don't think so. Many people in Bangkok will be in trouble if the government ③ ({ of / gets / stalls / rid / all } → ______________________________).

Huat: Because there are plenty of people who do not cook every day.

Kenta: You mean, people who live alone?

Bean: Yes, you can rarely find one room studio apartments with kitchens in Thailand.

Huat: Also, even if you have a kitchen, many people would think, "Why would you ④ (   ) (   ) for yourself after class or work when you can buy good food on the street? It's a waste of time and money."

Choose the picture that does not match the conversation and circle the number.

(1)

(2)

(3)

(4)

Column

文化を知るための Language：タイ語（ภาษาไทย）

ไม่เป็นไร「マイペンライ」

カフェで店員が注文していないものを持ってきたので、「注文と違いますが…」と言ったら、店員はどう返すでしょうか。日本では、まず「申し訳ございません」などの謝罪のことばですよね。でも、タイでは、こういう場合に「マイペンライ」と言われることがあります。

「マイペンライ」は「どういたしまして」や「大丈夫です」、または「気にしないで」という意味で主に使われる表現です。しかし、注文を間違った店員が使う「マイペンライ」のように、なかなか英語や日本語に訳すのが難しい場合もあります。

「マイペンライ」は、期待していた結果と違っていても取返しのつくことだったら「やり直せば済むので、気を悪くする必要はない」という意味で、気遣いのことばとして使われるそうです。たとえ自分のミスでも「あなたが気を揉む必要はないですよ」というタイ風の気遣いは、*the land of smiles*（微笑みの国）と称されるタイの人々のおおらかさを表しているとも言えるかもしれません。

Group Presentation

1. Which do you prefer, (A) or (B)? Put a check mark (✓) and write your reason in the box.

☐ (A) I prefer fragrant products.

☐ (B) I prefer odorless products.

Because ....

....

2. Make a group with two or three partners who have the same preference and present your thoughts. Write down the important key words in each box while listening to others.

Key words: Group member 1	Key words: Group member 2	Key words: Group member 3

3. Using your group member's key words, form one collective opinion.

....

....

....

4. Present your group's opinion to the class.

Unit 3

Germany: Leaders in Protecting Our Environment

ビールを愛する環境先進国ドイツとは！

Pre-Reading Activity

Look at picture 1. Guess what the men are wearing on their calves. Talk to your partner in English.

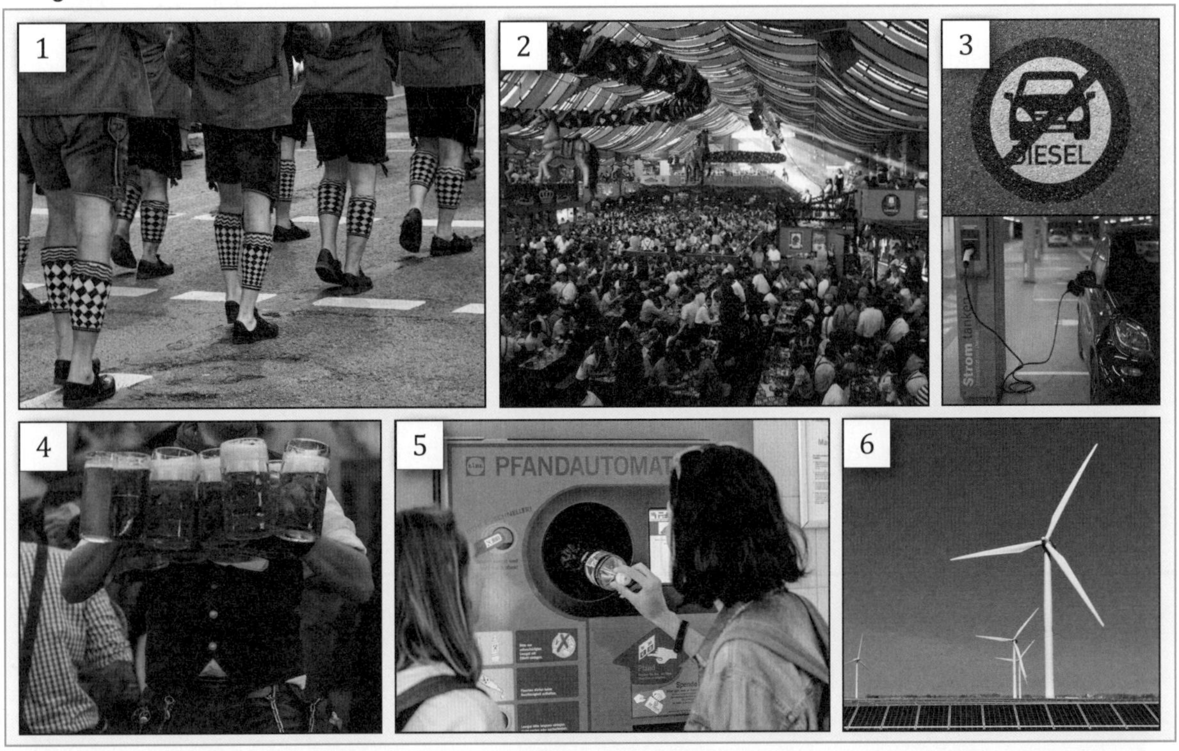

Vocabulary Map

Use the words in the box to complete the vocabulary map.

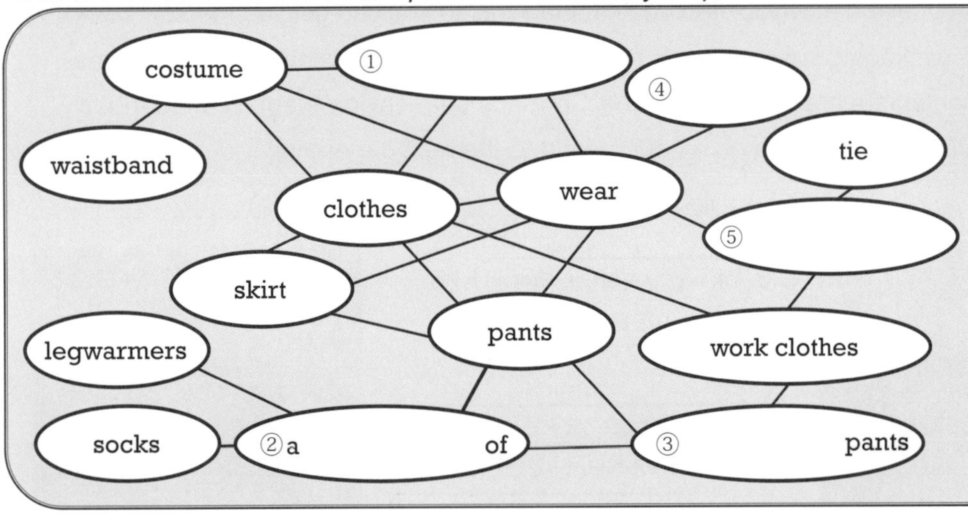

leather

pair

outfit

apron

wearer

Reading

Have you ever heard of the large beer festival and funfair in Germany, called *Oktoberfest*? The festival is held annually in Munich, Bavaria. *Oktoberfest* literally means "festival of October." The mayor of the city taps the first beer barrel and opens it while shouting, "*O'zapft is*!", which means "The barrel is open!" Everyone enjoys the special beers under the festival tents, and it is recommended to go in traditional Bavarian costume.

Women wear an outfit called a *dirndl*. It is a wide skirt with a tight waistband. According to tradition, if the *dirndl* wearer ties her apron to her right, she is married, engaged, or in love. If the apron is tied to the left, she is indicating that she is still available and probably unmarried. Men wear pants called *lederhosen*, which are knee-length leather pants worn with either a pair of patterned socks, or with a pair of legwarmers called *loferl*. These pants are usually work clothes. What is more, these traditional costumes are popular among young people to wear at *Oktoberfest*.

When you think of Germany, *Oktoberfest* and beer might not be the only things that come to mind. For those who are passionate about environmental issues, they must have heard about Germany's environmental protection policies. The German government has been tackling environmental issues for many years with political policies that encourage the citizens to work on protecting the environment. That is why the country tends to be seen as one of the leading environmentally conscious countries in the world. It is well-known that the German people usually do not like to waste things. Of course, not all of them are like that, but people outside Germany generally seem to have that kind of impression.

As a matter of fact, the recycling rate is three times more than Japan. They learn a lot about caring for the environment in school and have also developed a very effective system for recycling. For example, when you buy a drink in a plastic bottle or can, you pay a deposit for the container. The charge is added to the total cost of the drink. Most grocery stores have a recyclables collection machine so you can get your deposit back.

Moreover, packaging is eco-friendly as well. Paper-made containers, and now, grass and wood containers are being used. The Germans take environmental care seriously and are dedicated to passing on a better world to the next generation.

(404 words)

レダーホーセンを履いた男性と
ディルンドルを着た女性たち

ドイツのスーパーでよく見られる
リサイクルペーパーでできた野菜容器

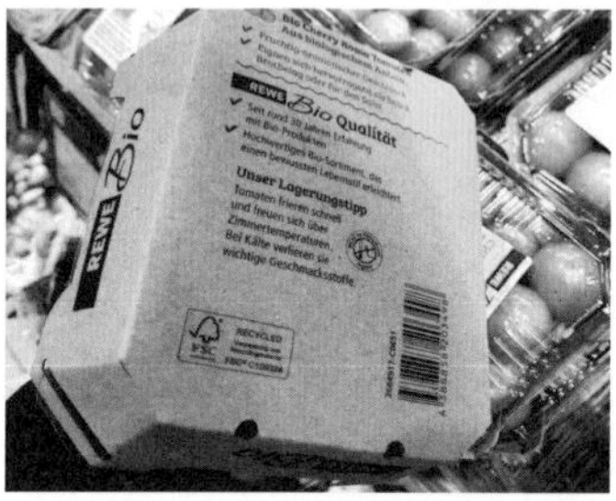

Find the following words in a dictionary and write their meanings in the parentheses below. Fill in the bracket with an appropriate word to complete the phrase.

Words and Phrases ★ 予習しておこう！

annually	(　　　　　　　)	a pair of~	(　　　　　　　)
literally	文字通りに	patterned	模様のある
mayor	町長、市長	come to mind	思い浮かぶ
beer barrel	ビールだる	be passionate about~	～に熱心だ
be recommended to ~	～ことが推奨される	environmental issue	(　　　　　　　)
costume	服装、衣装	protection	保護
outfit	(　　　　　　　)	tackle	（難問）に取り組む
according to ~	～によれば	political policy	政治方針
tie	結ぶ、くくる	conscious	(　　　　　　　)
apron	エプロン	impression	印象
engaged	婚約中の	[　　] a matter of fact	実際のところ
indicate	示す、意味する	recycling rate	リサイクル率
be available	交際相手がいない	deposit	内金、手付金
knee-length	ひざ丈の	recyclables	再生利用可能なもの
leather pants	革のズボン	be dedicated to~	～に全力を尽くす

Reading Exercises

A *You will hear three questions about the passage. Select the best answer and circle (A), (B) or (C).* 9

1. What does a *dirndl* say about a woman?
   (A) Where she is from
   (B) Whether she is in love or not
   (C) When she drinks beer

2.
   (A) Young people
   (B) The mayor
   (C) A lot of men

3.
   (A)
   (B)
   (C)

B *Circle the best choice to complete the following sentences.*

1. *Lederhosen* are knee-length leather pants _____ with a pair of patterned socks or with a pair of legwarmers.

(A) wear
(B) wearing
(C) worn
(D) wearer

2. Those who _____ environmental issues must have heard about Germany's environmental protection policies.

(A) have passionate on
(B) have passion against
(C) are passion beyond
(D) are passionate about

3. It is _____ that the German people usually do not like to waste things.

(A) clear-known
(B) hard-known
(C) deep-known
(D) well-known

4. The charge is added to the total _____ of the drink.

(A) cost
(B) fare
(C) salary
(D) toll

C *Based on the information in the passage, write "T" if it is true, or "F" if it is false.*

1. A woman tying the apron of her *dirndl* to her right probably has a lover. (　　)
2. *Oktoberfest* takes place in August and October. (　　)
3. In Germany, the recycling rate is higher than Japan. (　　)

D *Rearrange the words and phrases in the (　) to complete the sentences.*

1. オクトーバーフェストとビールのみが、思い浮かぶ唯一の物ではないかもしれない。
Oktoberfest and beer might not be (mind / that / to / things / come / the only).
Oktoberfest and beer might not be (______________________________
______________________________).

2. ドイツ人は次世代に、よりよい世界を残すことに全力を尽くしている。
The Germans (on / better / to / are / passing / a / dedicated) world to the next generation.
The Germans (______________________________
______________________________) world to the next generation.

Conversation

Listen to the conversation and answer the following. For ① and ③, fill in the blanks. For ②, put the words in the { } in the right order. For ④, choose the right words. 10

Kenta: Japanese hamburg steak is originally from Germany, isn't it? I've heard that the name "hamburg" ① ( ) ( ) the German city, Hamburg.

Daniel: Well, I first heard about it in Japan. Actually, I've never had hamburg steak in Germany.

Katarina: We have a big meatball dish, but it's not like Japanese hamburg steak.

Daniel: Ah, right. What we have is sautéed seasoned meatballs without any sauce on them.

Kenta: Really? That's so disappointing! I thought I could eat a genuine hamburg steak during my trip to Germany. Okay then. I just hope I can get some authentic baumkuchen.

Katarina: Oh, you won't see baumkuchen that much. It ② ({ to / quite / might / difficult / be } → ______________________)find shops that sell it.

Daniel: True. It is a German cake for sure. However, we see it in Japan much more often. I was amazed to learn that even Japanese convenience stores sold it.

Kenta: No way! Not that too! That is ③ ( ) ( ) disappointing! Please don't tell me sausages are rare in Germany!

Katarina: Don't worry, you can find a wide variety of sausages everywhere. ④ { Some of saved rice / Some are served sliced / Someone surfed sky } like ham, and others are eaten on bread.

Daniel: They grill them and serve them with rolls. They're a quick and easy German fast food.

Choose the picture that does not match the conversation and circle the number.

(1)

(2)

(3)

(4)

Column

文化を知るための Language：ドイツ語 (Deutsch)

Es geht um die Wurst. **「エス・ゲート・ウム・ディ・ヴルストゥ」**

ソーセージはドイツ国民の生活に欠かせない食材ですが、ドイツにはソーセージを使った表現もたくさんあります。*Es geht um die Wurst.* は直訳すると「ソーセージが問題だ」ですが、「今が正念場だ」、「最善を尽くすときだ」という意味で使われます。これは昔、お祭りのコンテストなどの景品がソーセージだったことに由来しているそうです。また、丁寧ではない言い回しですが、*Das ist mir Wurst.*（私にとってはソーセージだ）は、「そんなことはどうでもいい」という意味になるそうです。

他にも、「特別扱いされる」という意味で使われる *Eine Extrawurst kriegen.*（必要以上のソーセージを手に入れる）など、ドイツ語ではソーセージが言語の中でも大活躍しています。このように日常で多用する慣用表現やことわざにソーセージが頻繁に現れることからも、ソーセージがいかにドイツ人の生活に欠かせない物なのかということが見えてきます。

Group Presentation

1. Which do you prefer, (A) or (B)? Put a check mark (✓) and write your reason in the box.

☐ (A) We should have more recycling bins to protect the environment.

☐ (B) We should have a system that pays you for recycling to protect the environment.

Because ....

....

2. Make a group with two or three partners who have the same preference and present your thoughts. Write down the important key words in each box while listening to others.

Key words: Group member 1	Key words: Group member 2	Key words: Group member 3

3. Using your group member's key words, form one collective opinion.

....

....

....

4. Present your group's opinion to the class.

Unit 4

Turkey: Finish Up Your Coffee

コーヒーとお茶がつなぐ人情文化とは！

Pre-Reading Activity

Look at picture 2. Guess what the person is doing. Talk to your partner in English.

Vocabulary Map

Use the words in the box to complete the vocabulary map.

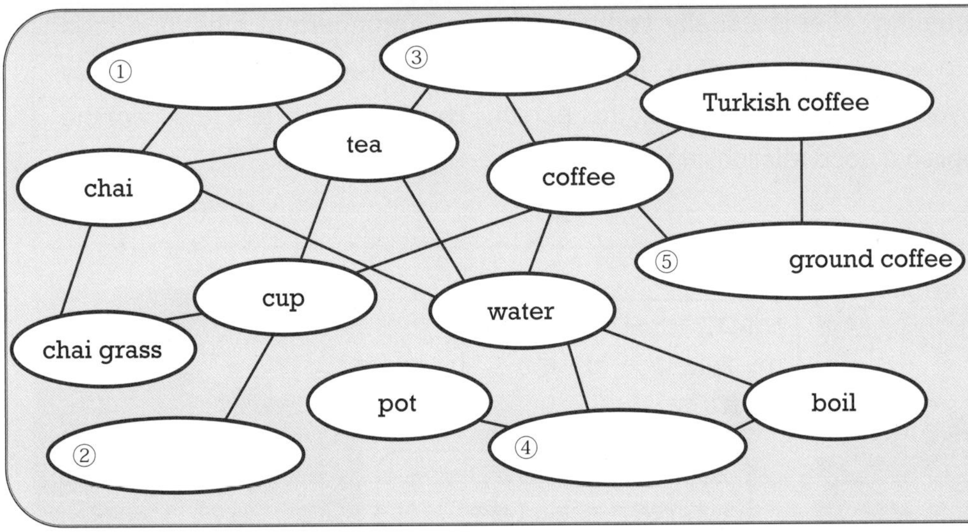

kettle

brew

finely

leaves

saucer

Reading

11

Turkey is deeply associated with tea and coffee. Just as Japanese people drink tea daily, so do Turkish people. According to a survey, Turkey consumes the most tea in the world. They consume three times more tea than the Japanese do!

Chai is a type of tea enjoyed in Turkey that is typically served in a small cup. The kettle used to prepare it is called a *caydanlik*. It is a uniquely shaped, two-tiered kettle found in Turkish homes. Tea leaves are added into the upper tier of the kettle, and water is added into the bottom tier. When the water begins to boil, it is poured into the upper tier, allowed to steep, then poured into a chai glass.

Coffee is also important in Turkey. In 2013, Turkish coffee was registered as a UNESCO Intangible Cultural Heritage (ICH), under the name of “Turkish coffee culture and tradition,” alongside Japanese *washoku*. As you can guess by its official ICH name, coffee has a strong connection to Turkish culture. In fact, it is so important to their culture that it is said that a wife is expected to be able to brew a good cup of coffee.

To make a traditional cup of Turkish coffee, a special pot called a *cezve*, which looks like a ladle, is used. Water and finely ground coffee are added, then it is placed on top of a flame. After the coffee boils, it is poured into a cup, unfiltered. In case you may be wondering, you do not drink the coffee grounds! Let them settle at the bottom and drink the coffee on top.

It is customary to read someone’s fortune with the leftover coffee grounds. A saucer is placed on top of the cup, then they are both flipped. The grounds are left to cool, and the cup is removed. The coffee grounds will have trails and marks left in them, which are then used to tell your fortune. This has some similarities to *chabashira*, the Japanese practice of finding good fortune through tea leaves.

Coffee can also signify the importance of a relationship. For example, in a regular business meeting, chai is usually served, however, in important meetings, it is customary to serve Turkish coffee. If you are offered a Turkish coffee, this likely means that you have gained trust from that person. Thus, it is important to accept the offer to establish a good relationship.

(403 words)

トルココーヒーを飲み終え、カップの上にソーサーをかぶせて裏返す

カップの内側の底に付いたコーヒーかすの模様で占いをする様子

Find the following words in a dictionary and write their meanings in the parentheses below. Fill in the bracket with an appropriate word to complete the phrase.

Words and Phrases ★ 予習しておこう！

be associated [ ] ~	～と結びついている	unfiltered	ろ過されない
just as ~	まさに～のように	grounds	コーヒーかす
survey	( )	it is customary to ~	習慣的に～をする
serve	（飲食物を）出す	read one's fortune	～の運勢を見る
kettle	( )	saucer	受け皿、ソーサー
uniquely shaped	独特な形をした	flip	( )
two-tiered	2層になった	cool	冷やす
boil	( )	similarity to ~	～との類似点
steep	（液体に）浸す	practice	慣例
register	登録する	signify	示す、意味する
Intangible Cultural Heritage	無形文化遺産	offer	（飲食物などを）提供する、提供
brew	( )	likely	おそらく
pot	深鍋	gain trust	信頼を得る
finely ground	細かく挽いた	establish	確立する

Reading Exercises

A *You will hear three questions about the passage. Select the best answer and circle (A), (B) or (C).* 12

1. Why are Turkish traditional kettles unique?
   (A) They are used more often in Japan.
   (B) They have a special way of coffee making.
   (C) They have a two-tiered design.

2.
   (A) They were registered
   (B) They are traditional
   (C) They are served

3.
   (A)
   (B)
   (C)

B *Circle the best choice to complete the following sentences.*

1. Turkey is deeply associated _____ tea and coffee.

(A) with
(B) over
(C) behind
(D) inside

2. Chai is a type of tea enjoyed in Turkey that is _____ served in a small cup.

(A) type
(B) typical
(C) typically
(D) typing

3. After the cup and the saucer are flipped, the grounds are left to cool and the cup _____.

(A) remove
(B) is removed
(C) is removing
(D) had removed

4. If you are offered a Turkish coffee, this likely means that you have gained _____.

(A) mind
(B) notice
(C) belief
(D) trust

C *Based on the information in the passage, write "T" if it is true, or "F" if it is false.*

1. Turkish people drink tea a lot more than Japanese people. (　　)
2. When you use a *caydanlik*, you should put water into the bottom tier. (　　)
3. Chai is an Intangible Cultural Heritage in Turkey. (　　)

D *Rearrange the words and phrases in the (　) to complete the sentences.*

1. トルコ人は日本人の 3 倍多くお茶を消費する。
Turkish people consume (three / the Japanese / than / tea / more / times) do.
Turkish people consume (____
____) do.

2. 不思議に思っているといけないので言っておくが、コーヒーかすは飲まない。
(may / case / wondering / you / be / in), you do not drink the coffee grounds.
(____
______________________________), you do not drink the coffee grounds.

Conversation

Listen to the conversation and answer the following. For ①, choose the right words. For ② and ③, fill in the blanks. For ④, put the words in the { } in the right order. 13

Kenta: Turkish ice cream is famous here in Japan. Is it popular in Turkey, too?

Onur: Sure, it is. Actually, in Turkey, we call the ice cream *dondurma*, but the word means any ① { kids of / kind soap / kind of } ice cream.

Kenta: I've seen it served at a food stall, and I wonder, why is it so ② (   ) ?

Ayse: Good question. It is important to the performances done when serving it, but it is originally because of the weather in Turkey.

Onur: In some places in Turkey, it gets over 40 degrees, so they made the ice cream thick and gooey so that it doesn't melt easily.

Kenta: So it's like a heat-resistant ice cream!

Ayse: ③ (   ) (   ) Turkish food, isn't it amazing to see doner kebabs in food stalls?

Kenta: Yeah, the big rotating piece of meat that they shred!

Ayse: Right. The word "doner" is from the Turkish *döner*, which means "rotate."

Onur: They originally only used mutton, but nowadays, they use beef or chicken, too. Did you know the gigantic meat is actually made of many layers of thin meat?

Kenta: Really? I thought they just cooked ④ ({ of / whole / beef / a / piece } →
____) !

Choose the picture that does not match the conversation and circle the number.

(1)

(2)

(3)

(4)

Column

文化を知るための Language：トルコ語（Türkçe）

Bır fincan kahvenin kırk yıl hatırı var

「ビル・フィンジャン・カフヴェニン・クルク・ユル・ハトゥル・ヴァル」

日本には「一期一会」ということばがあり、これは「いつも『この人と会うのは最初で最後かも』という心構えで、人との出会いを大切にしなさい」という意味で、茶道に由来することばです。

一方、トルコ語には「1 杯のコーヒーが 40 年間記憶に残る」という、コーヒーを使って人との交流の大事さを説くことばがあります。「40 年」という数字があるのは、トルコでは 40 が「とてもたくさん」という比喩になるためです。これは、日本語で「100 年の恋も冷める」の 100 や、「八百万《やおよろず》の神」の 800 万という数字が「とても多い」のたとえで使われるのと似ています。

つまり「40 年の記憶」は「長年の記憶」と解釈でき、全体的には「人とコーヒーを飲みながら得た思い出は、互いの心にいつまでも残るだろう」という意味になります。このことからも、コーヒーがトルコの人々の生活に深く根付き、コミュニケーションの重要な役割を担っていることがわかります。

Group Presentation

1. Which do you prefer, (A) or (B)? Put a check mark (✓) and write your reason in the box.

☐(A) On your overseas trip, you would accept a drink from a stranger sitting next to you.

☐(B) On your overseas trip, you would not accept a drink from a stranger sitting next to you.

Because ……………………………………………………………………………………

……………………………………………………………………………………………

2. Make a group with two or three partners who have the same preference and present your thoughts. Write down the important key words in each box while listening to others.

Key words: Group member 1	Key words: Group member 2	Key words: Group member 3

3. Using your group member's key words, form one collective opinion.

……………………………………………………………………………………………

……………………………………………………………………………………………

……………………………………………………………………………………………

4. Present your group's opinion to the class.

Unit 5

Russia: Home to the Coldest Place Inhabited by Humans

極寒の中に生きる文化とは！

Pre-Reading Activity

Look at picture 1. Guess what the children are doing. Talk to your partner in English.

Vocabulary Map

Use the words in the box to complete the vocabulary map.

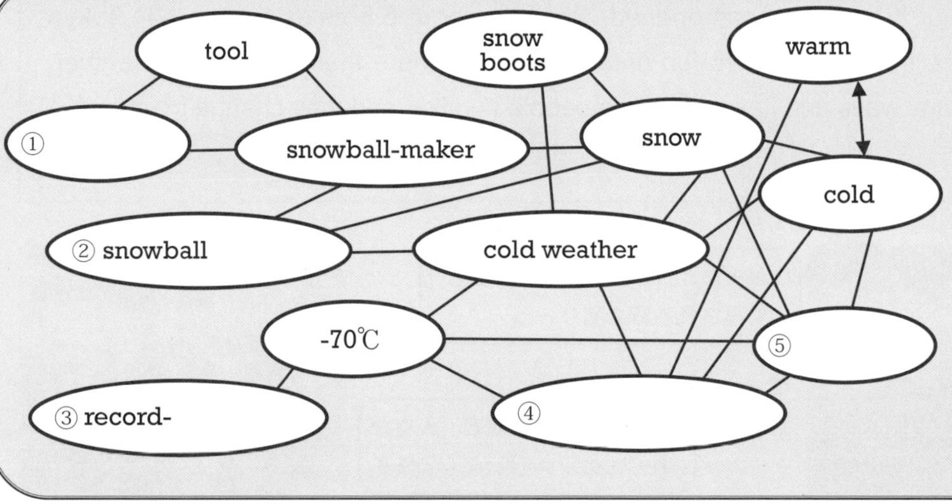

device
breaking
freezing
fight
temperature

Reading

14

Russia is a very cold country. For example, in the town called Oymyakon, the average temperature can go below -50 degrees Celsius in the winter, and the town was hit by record-breaking cold weather at -70 degrees in 1992. To live in such freezing conditions, people in Russia created practical items such as *valenki*, traditional woolen boots. They are lighter than regular snow boots and have a warmth insulation system that keeps the inside warm, even in temperatures of -30 degrees.

Vodka is a longtime friend for adults to keep themselves warm on the inside. Vodka is a kind of distilled spirit, like tequila and gin. It is essential to make cocktails and is loved all over the world. The liquor is flavorless and scentless, and the average alcohol content is 40 percent. Just like Japan has a large selection of sakes, Russia has a wide variety of vodkas. When it comes to drinking snacks, Russians used to enjoy caviar, but now tend to like cured slabs of pork fat called *salo*, which look like sliced bacon.

Children also enjoy the cold weather by having snowball fights with friends. However, when they are outside making a snowball, their hands get really cold. In this case, they use a snowball maker. With this plastic, scissor-like device, they can make a snowball just by squeezing the handles. Even little children who have a weak grip can make a perfect snowball in the blink of an eye. Thus, a snowball-maker is an important tool to win the fight.

Russians have long appreciated items that can make their lives easier and more fun in the cold weather. However, there are always some traditions that stay, and also some new trends that come in. For instance, it is so cold in Russia that they even have a traditional festival, *Maslenitsa*, that celebrates the end of winter. In the festival, you will see people enjoying singing, dancing and eating outside; and even having snowball fights and burning traditional dolls. On the other hand, recently, Russians are becoming more health-conscious and are drinking less vodka. Also, in Moscow, a giant indoor theme-park has opened, which is about 6.5 times bigger than Tokyo Dome, where people can have fun under the roof. Where there is freezing weather, there are many ways and items that help people survive, and they change over time.

(394 words)

ウォッカと、そのおつまみとして
よく食される豚の脂サーラ

伝統的な衣装を着て、人々が
マースレニツァを祝っている様子

Find the following words in a dictionary and write their meanings in the parentheses below. Fill in the bracket with an appropriate word to complete the phrase.

Words and Phrases ★ 予習しておこう！

temperature	気温	drinking snack	おつまみ
record-breaking	記録を破る、新記録の	cured	くん製の
freezing	(　　　　　　)	slab	厚切り
practical	実用的な	pork fat	豚肉の脂肪
woolen	羊毛の、ウール製の	snowball fight	(　　　　　　)
insulation	分離、断熱	scissor-like	ハサミのような
longtime friend	長年の友人、旧友	device	道具、装置
distilled	蒸留された	squeeze	握る
spirits	蒸留酒	handle	取っ手
essential	(　　　　　　)	grip	握力
liquor	（特に蒸留の）酒	in the blink of an eye	瞬く間に、一瞬で
flavorless	味のない	tool	道具、用具
alcohol content	(　　　　　　)	appreciate	ありがたく思う
large selection	豊富な品揃え	health-conscious	(　　　　　　)
when it comes [　　] ~	～に関して言えば	over time	時が経つにつれて

Reading Exercises

A *You will hear three questions about the passage. Select the best answer and circle (A), (B) or (C).* 15

1. What do people do in *Maslenitsa*?
   (A) They appreciate the freezing weather.
   (B) They drink a lot of special alcohol.
   (C) They celebrate the change of seasons.

2.
   (A) They are
   (B) They go
   (C) They keep

3.
   (A)
   (B)
   (C)

B *Circle the best choice to complete the following sentences.*

1. The town was _____ by record-breaking cold weather.

(A) hit
(B) strike
(C) beat
(D) kick

2. Japan has a _____ selection of sakes.

(A) deep
(B) large
(C) high
(D) much

3. Even little children can make a perfect snowball in the _____.

(A) ball of an eye
(B) close of an eye
(C) side of an eye
(D) blink of an eye

4. A giant theme-park opened in Moscow, _____ people can have fun under the roof.

(A) which
(B) whose
(C) where
(D) when

C *Based on the information in the passage, write "T" if it is true, or "F" if it is false.*

1. Vodka has a strong flavor like tequila or gin. (　　)
2. Some snowball makers have a similar appearance to scissors. (　　)
3. How Russians deal with the cold weather is completely the same as the old days. (　　)

D *Rearrange the words and phrases in the (　) to complete the sentences.*

1. ヴァレンキというスノーブーツには、内側を保温する防寒システムがある。
The snow boots called *valenki* have a warmth (warm / keeps / that / the inside / system / insulation).
The snow boots called *valenki* have a warmth (____
____).

2. ロシア人はより健康に気をつかうようになり、ウォッカの飲酒量も減っている。
Russians are becoming (less / more / and / are / drinking / health-conscious) vodka.
Russians are becoming (____
____) vodka.

Conversation

Listen to the conversation and answer the following. For ① and ④, fill in the blanks. For ②, put the words in the { } in the right order. For ③, choose the right words. 16

Kenta: It's freezing. I'd like to have that Russian red soup we had before.

Nicolay: You mean borscht, right? You're ① (   ) (   ) Russian food! But did you know Russian and French cuisine are connected? For example, when you hear of a course meal, you probably imagine French cuisine, don't you?

Kenta: Yes, and it sounds expensive, too.

Nicolay: Right? But people say that its origin was actually from Russia. Russia is cold, so they started to ② ({ time / the / at / serve / one / a / dishes } → ____________________) to eat while they're hot.

Yuliya: In fact, some Japanese sea foods also relate to Russian food.

Kenta: Wait! I know that! I've heard that the word *ikura* is Russian.

Yuliya: ③ { Boo to I / Bull's eye / Boots guy } ! *Ikura* commonly means "fish roe" in Russian, so both salmon roe and caviar are *ikura*.

Kenta: Caviar is *ikura*?! That's so confusing!

Nicolay: This might ④ (   ) (   ) too. We often eat bread in Russia, but our bread is mostly black! Not because it's chocolate-mixed, but because it's rye bread.

Yuliya: Yes, it's not like the white bread you eat in Japan. You should try *borodinsky*. It's a traditional dark brown bread and very popular in Russia.

Choose the picture that does not match the conversation and circle the number.

(1)

(2)

(3)

(4)

Column

文化を知るための Language：ロシア語（русский）

Ничего「ニチェボ」

ロシアの日常会話でよく使われる表現のひとつに「ニチェボ」があります。「なんとかなるさ、そんなこと気にしなくていいよ」といった意味で、親しい者同士の会話では「スパシーバ（ありがとう）」への返答としても使えます。英語でいうなら *Don't worry.* や *No problem.* にあたり、さらにはタイ語の「マンペンライ」（Unit 2 のコラム参照）と似た表現とも言われています。

この表現は様々な状況で使うことができます。たとえば、多少のミスや心配ごとに対してはもちろんですが、重要な会議で飲み物をこぼすなど、日本人には大事件とも思える出来事に対しても「ニチェボー！」のように使われることがあります。このようなことから、ロシアの人々の考え方や文化を、ニチェボ主義、ニチェボ精神、ニチェボ文化、などと呼ぶこともあります。

ことばひとつですべてのミスをなかったことにはできませんが、細かなことを気にしがちな人は、時にはこれくらいのおおらかな気持ちで物事を考えるといいかもしれません。

Group Presentation

1. Which do you prefer, (A) or (B)? Put a check mark (✓) and write your reason in the box.

☐ (A) If I studied abroad, I would choose an extremely hot place.

☐ (B) If I studied abroad, I would choose an extremely cold place.

Because ……………………………………………………………………………

……………………………………………………………………………………

2. Make a group with two or three partners who have the same preference and present your thoughts. Write down the important key words in each box while listening to others.

Key words: Group member 1	Key words: Group member 2	Key words: Group member 3

3. Using your group member's key words, form one collective opinion.

……………………………………………………………………………………

……………………………………………………………………………………

……………………………………………………………………………………

4. Present your group's opinion to the class.

Unit 6

Israel: A Land of Tradition and Technology

伝統と技術が融合する文化とは！

Pre-Reading Activity

Look at picture 2. Guess what the round things on their heads are for. Talk to your partner in English.

Vocabulary Map

Use the words in the box to complete the vocabulary map.

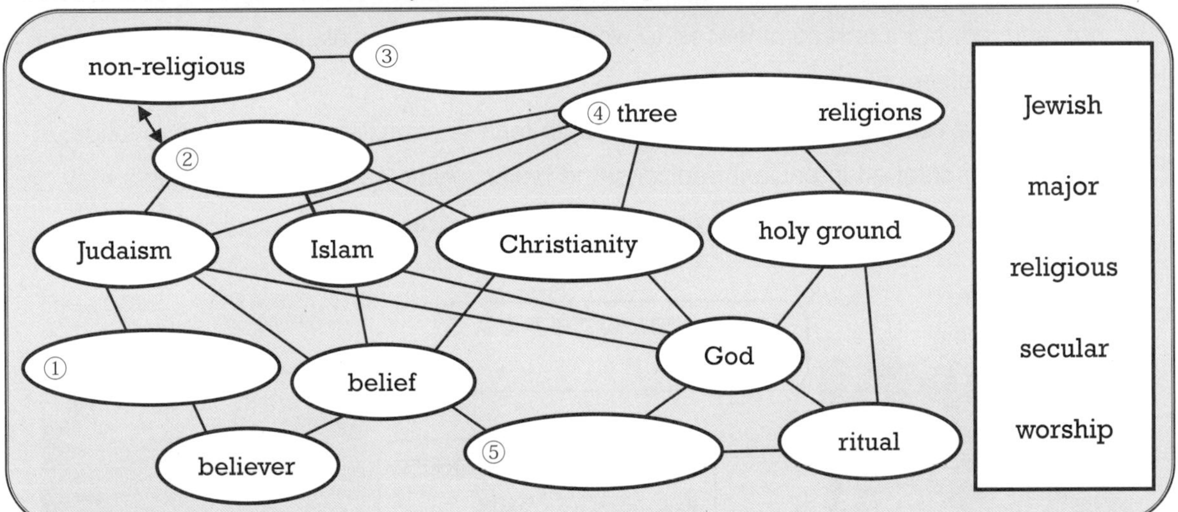

Reading

17

When you think of cutting-edge technologies, you may think of Silicon Valley, home to Apple, Facebook, Google, and many more. But did you know that Israel is also home to great technological innovation? You may think of Israel as being the holy ground for the three major religions of Judaism, Christianity, and Islam. Not only that, Israel has brought many innovations such as CPU development, instant messaging, drones, and so on. From a young age, Israeli students learn how to program. There are world-renowned universities and institutes of technology in the country.

Israeli people also get a lot of hands-on experience with advanced technology through their military service. High school graduates must serve in the military. Boys must serve nearly three years, and girls must serve two. Many of these soldiers are required to stay at a dormitory but can go home on the weekends. You will often see some young soldiers returning home, carrying their rifles.

Religion is one of the foundations of Israeli culture and lifestyle. Israel has the highest number of Jewish citizens. However, that does not mean that everyone follows Jewish law. In general, Jewish Israelis can be divided into three types, those who are orthodox, conservative, and secular. Orthodox Jews are very strict about following Jewish law. They are not living in a world of technology and try not to be involved in the secular world. Conservative Jews live part of their lives outside of the religion; however, religion still plays a large role in their lives. Secular Jews are more open to the rest of the society. They do not deny the religion, but they seem to have more personal freedom on a daily basis.

It is often difficult to avoid religious traditions in Israel. For instance, you should ask if an Israeli person can eat fish without scales, or pork, because they are not allowed by Jewish law. Also, you will see men wearing a small cap on their head called a *kippah*. It is a reminder to people that God is always over them. For the non-religious, it is not required, but it is recommended to wear one at a ritual or place of worship, out of respect for other believers.

Israel is a country of two sides: one of high-tech accomplishments and innovation, and another steeped in ancient traditions and beliefs. Although these two aspects may seem at odds with each other, they coexist perfectly in Israel.

(406 words)

エルサレム旧市街で任務に就く
若い女性兵士たち

テクノロジーを駆使した砂漠での
農業。写真はぶどう栽培

Find the following words in a dictionary and write their meanings in the parentheses below. Fill in the bracket with an appropriate word to complete the phrase.

Words and Phrases ★ 予習しておこう！

cutting-edge	最先端の	dormitory	寮
home	本拠地、発祥地	foundation	土台、基礎
innovation	革新、新手法	Jewish	ユダヤ人の、ユダヤ系の
holy ground	(　　　　) 場所	orthodox	(宗教上) 正統派の
three major ~	3 大〜	secular	宗教色のない
Judaism	(　　　　)	on a daily basis	日常的に
Christianity	(　　　　)	religious	(　　　　)
Islam	イスラム教	[　　] instance	たとえば
development	開発	ritual	儀式、儀式的行事
world-renowned	世界的に有名な	worship	(　　　　)
institute of technology	工科大学	accomplishment	業績
hands-on	実地の、実践の	steeped in	深く浸透している
advanced	先進的な、進んだ	ancient	古くからの、古代の
military service	兵役	aspect	(もの・ことの) 面
be required	義務付けられる	coexist	共存する

Reading Exercises

A *You will hear three questions about the passage. Select the best answer and circle (A), (B) or (C).* 18

1. What do Israeli people have to do after high school?
   (A) Learn how to program
   (B) Change their lifestyle
   (C) Serve in the military

2.
   (A) To develop
   (B) To carry
   (C) To eat

3.
   (A)
   (B)
   (C)

B *Circle the best choice to complete the following sentences.*

1. Israeli people also get a lot of _____ experience with advanced technology.

(A) hand-hot
(B) hand-in
(C) hands-on
(D) hand-blown

2. Israel has the _____ number of Jewish citizens.

(A) hugest
(B) widest
(C) most
(D) largest

3. In general, Jewish Israelis can be _____ three types.

(A) belonged to
(B) divided into
(C) made up for
(D) brought about

4. Israel is a country of two sides, and one side is steeped _____ ancient traditions and beliefs.

(A) in
(B) over
(C) off
(D) behind

C *Based on the information in the passage, write "T" if it is true, or "F" if it is false.*

1. Judaism is one of the three major religions in the world. (　　)
2. Young soldiers staying at a dormitory may go home at times. (　　)
3. Secular Jews are people who do not accept religion at all. (　　)

D *Rearrange the words and phrases in the (　) to complete the sentences.*

1. 正統派のユダヤ人は、無宗教の世界とは関わらないようにしている。
Orthodox Jews (be / not / involved / to / try / in) the secular world.
Orthodox Jews (____
____________________________) the secular world.

2. 頭の上にキッパーと呼ばれる小さな帽子をかぶっている男性たちを目にするだろう。
You will see (their / on / small / a / men / cap / wearing) head called a *kippah*.
You will see (____
____________________________) head called a *kippah*.

Conversation

Listen to the conversation and answer the following. For ①, choose the right words. For ③, put the words in the { } in the right order. For ② and ④, fill in the blanks. 19

Kenta: ① { How's it / How come / How can } there are two sinks and dishwashers in the kitchen in this photo?

Tamar: Oh, I took that photo at my parents' house in Israel. My parents are conservative.

Kenta: Conservative Jew means a very ② ( ) Jewish person, right? But, is that related to having two sinks and dishwashers in a kitchen?

Guy: Have you ever heard of *kosher* laws? These are rules about food and eating conditions that must follow Jewish law.

Kenta: Yes, I've heard of it. You cannot eat pork, fish without fins and scales, and other things like shrimp and crab, right?

Tamar: That's correct. There ③ ({ also / where / is / rule / a } → ____________________) you can't mix dairy products and meat. My parents follow *kosher* rules.

Guy: So they need two kinds of plates, cutlery, sinks, and dishwashers.

Tamar: You must separate those two things, too.

Kenta: Wait. Guy, weren't you eating lasagna the other day ④ ( ) ( ) you are Jewish? That contains meat, milk and cheese!

Guy: I don't eat *kosher*. However, I don't want to eat pork. It's probably because I've never had it since I was born.

Choose the picture that does not match the conversation and circle the number.

(1)

(2)

(3)

(4)

Column

文化を知るためのLanguage：ヘブライ語 (עברית)

שלום **「シャローム」**

イスラエルで話されているのはイスラエル語ではなく、ヘブライ語という言語です。ヘブライ語は紀元前の旧約聖書の時代に話されていたユダヤ人の言語ですが、ユダヤ人はローマ帝国に国を滅ぼされ、世界のあちこちに拡散してしまい、西暦200年頃にヘブライ語は話しことばとしては世の中から消えてしまいました。ところが、ユダヤ人の間で故郷を再建しようという運動が起こり、約1700年の時を経て、話しことばとして現代ヘブライ語が復活したのです。一度、滅亡した言語が復活し、日常で話されるようになったという例は、ヘブライ語が歴史上唯一の言語になります。

「シャローム」は朝でも昼でも夜でも使える英語の *Hello.* に当たることばですが、「シャローム」には「平和」という意味もあります。イスラエルでは金曜日の日没から土曜日の日没までが安息日です。金曜日には「シャバット・シャローム」（平和な安息日を）というあいさつで人々とお別れをし、安息日を迎えます。

Group Presentation

1. Which do you prefer, (A) or (B)? Put a check mark (✓) and write your reason in the box.

☐ (A) A society that gives more importance to tradition than convenience.

☐ (B) A society that only pursues technology.

Because ....

....

2. Make a group with two or three partners who have the same preference and present your thoughts. Write down the important key words in each box while listening to others.

Key words: Group member 1	Key words: Group member 2	Key words: Group member 3

3. Using your group member's key words, form one collective opinion.

....

....

....

4. Present your group's opinion to the class.

Unit 7

South Africa: The Country with 11 Different Names

アフリカ大陸最南端の親睦文化とは！

Pre-Reading Activity

Look at picture 2. Guess what the item is. Talk to your partner in English.

1

2

3

4

5

6

7

Vocabulary Map

Use the words in the box to complete the vocabulary map.

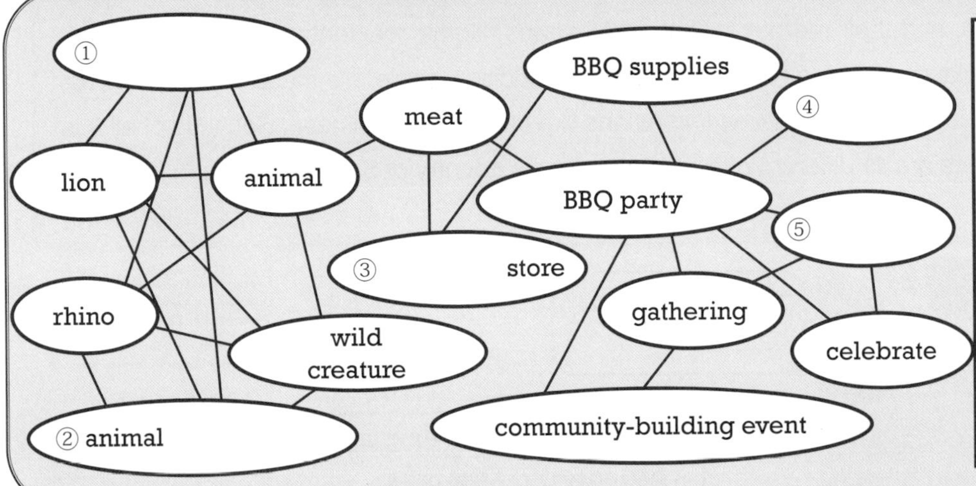

- grocery
- charcoal
- beast
- feast
- sanctuary

Reading

20

What is South Africa like? You may imagine animals such as lions and giraffes. In animal sanctuaries, there are a great variety of beasts such as jaguars, elephants, rhinos, and so on. If you travel to the seaside of Cape Town, you can even find penguins there. Also, you might think that they roam freely around the towns, but that is not the case; the people of South Africa do not really live among these animals. Not all the country is full of magnificent nature or wild creatures.

In South Africa, there was an old legislation called "apartheid". It was a system of law that supported segregation policies against the non-white people of South Africa. It lasted for about 50 years, starting in 1948 and ending in 1991. Because of this, some may assume that South Africans have closed minds, but in reality, a lot of modern-day South Africans are easy going and friendly.

They may ask you to come to a barbeque party, called *Braai*, for the weekend if you become friends. Most houses in South Africa have equipment for *Braai* installed in their gardens or balconies so they can enjoy a gathering with family or friends almost every weekend, all-year-round. They have a holiday known as National Braai Day. It is a day set aside for all South Africans to celebrate their rich heritage. When they have something to celebrate, big or small, they light fires and prepare great barbeque feasts. As one can imagine, they have no trouble finding charcoal and other barbeque supplies in grocery stores throughout the year. Generally, the food served is all about meat like beef, pork, chicken, and huge South African sausages called *boerewors*. Even after eating barbeque, people enjoy chatting and relaxing. After all, *Braai* is a traditional, community-building event.

South Africa is a mixed-race nation. They have 11 official languages. The black residents make up the majority of the nation. They include members from the Zulu and Xhosa tribe, and they speak different languages. There are also Caucasians who originated from the Netherlands, and their mother tongue is Afrikaans. Some residents trace their heritage back to England and speak English natively. In addition, there are those who are mixed-race called colored. You will even find Asians like Indians and Chinese. Because of all this diversity, there are 11 different official names for the country of South Africa!

(398 words)

ブラーイを囲む人々。
肉の種類は様々

南アフリカで最も多くの人々に使用される
5言語が使われている国家の歌詞

Find the following words in a dictionary and write their meanings in the parentheses below. Fill in the bracket with an appropriate word to complete the phrase.

Words and Phrases ★ 予習しておこう！

animal sanctuary	( )	heritage	（受け継がれた）伝統
a great variety [ ] ~	多種多様な～	light fires	火をつける
beast	（大型で危険な）動物	feast	祝宴、ごちそう
roam	歩き回る、放浪する	charcoal	木炭、炭
magnificent	壮大な、すばらしい	supply	必需品、用品
wild creature	( )	grocery store	( )
legislation	法律	chat	おしゃべりする
apartheid	アパルトヘイト	mixed-race	人種が入り交じった
segregation policy	隔離政策	resident	住民、市民
assume that ~	当然～と思う	tribe	部族
closed mind	排他的な考え	Caucasian	( )
equipment	装置、装備	originated from	～に起源がある
installed	設置された	mother tongue	母語
all-year-round	一年中	trace ... back to ~	…が～にさかのぼる
set aside	確保する	diversity	( )

Reading Exercises

A *You will hear three questions about the passage. Select the best answer and circle (A), (B) or (C).* 21

1. Which is one of the purposes of *Braai*?
   (A) To raise money for poor people
   (B) To save endangered wild creatures
   (C) To establish a good relationship among the community

2.
   (A) Enjoy
   (B) Enjoy
   (C) Enjoy

3.
   (A)
   (B)
   (C)

B Circle the best choice to complete the following sentences.

1. There are a great _____ of beasts such as jaguars, elephants, rhinos, and so on.

(A) varies
(B) various
(C) variety
(D) varieties

2. You might think that animals roam freely around the towns, but that is not _____.

(A) the fun
(B) the case
(C) the even
(D) the fiction

3. They _____ fires and prepare great BBQ feasts.

(A) light
(B) bright
(C) weight
(D) might

4. Their _____ tongue is Afrikaans.

(A) mouth
(B) talking
(C) mother
(D) original

C Based on the information in the passage, write "T" if it is true, or "F" if it is false.

1. A lot of different types of wild creatures can be seen in animal sanctuaries. (　　)
2. Many people in South Africa go to camp sites for BBQ every weekend. (　　)
3. There are more black residents than white residents in South Africa. (　　)

D Rearrange the words and phrases in the (　) to complete the sentences.

1. 南アフリカのほとんどの家には庭やバルコニーに設置されたBraai用の装置がある。
Most houses in South Africa (Braai / in / have / installed / equipment / for) their gardens or balconies.
Most houses in South Africa (______________________________
______________________________) their gardens or balconies.

2. 彼らは1年中、食料品店でバーベキュー用品を難なく見つけられる。
They have (no / BBQ / finding / grocery / supplies / in / trouble) stores throughout the year.
They have (______________________________
______________________________) stores throughout the year.

Conversation

Listen to the conversation and answer the following. For ①, put the words in the { } in the right order. For ② and ④, fill in the blanks. For ③,choose the right words. 22

Zach: Take a look at this photo. This is my sister who lives in South Africa.

Kenta: She looks exactly like you! By the way, what is she eating? It looks like a huge curry bread! It looks really good!

Janet: Oh, that's *Bunny Chow,* a very popular fast food in South Africa. You ① ({ half / the / of / scoop / inside / out } → ______________________________) a loaf of bread and fill it with Indian curry. You dip the removed bread into the curry.

Zach: There are different varieties of curries such as mutton, lamb, chicken, cheese, peas... *Bunny Chow* was ② (   ) (   ) Indian South Africans of Durban. So, it's truly an Indian dish but you probably won't find it in India.

Kenta: It looks so good! I definitely want to try it.

Janet: You've got to try this sandwich! The *Gatsby*! It's a signature sandwich in Cape Town.

Kenta: *Gatsby*? Wasn't there some movie with that name?

Zach: Yes, *The Great Gatsby* from the 70's. The sandwich was named after it.

Kenta: Tell me more!

Janet: It's a roll with ③ { various fillings / values feedings / very athletics } like steak, fried eggs and salad. But what's important is that you put French fries in it.

Zach: And ④ (   ), our portions are pretty big!

Choose the picture that does not match the conversation and circle the number.

(1)

(2)

(3)

(4)

Column

文化を知るための Language：アフリカーンス語 (Afrikaans)

***seekoei*「シアクゥイ」／*leeu*「リィーウ」**

南アフリカの 11 ある公用語の中の一つにアフリカーンスという言語があります。様々な野生動物が生息する国の言語だけあって、アフリカーンスの慣用句にはアフリカならではの動物が多く登場します。例えば、アフリカーンスで「それは *seekoei*（カバ）の耳にすぎない」という表現がありますが、どんな意味か想像できるでしょうか。これは「氷山の一角」という意味で、水中にもぐったカバの耳だけが水面から出ている様子がイメージできます。また、「短い棒で *leeu*（ライオン）の睾丸を引っかく」という言い回しがありますが、こちらは「けんかを売る」という意味で使われます。

「アフリカーンス語」と聞くと、アフリカ古来の言語にも思えますが、オランダ語から派生したゲルマン語派（英語やドイツ語と同じグループ）の言語で、ヨーロッパ系の言語では最も新しくできた言語です。ズールー語、コサ語に次いで南アフリカで３番目に母語話者が多い言語になります。

Group Presentation

1. Which do you prefer, (A) or (B)? Put a check mark (✓) and write your reason in the box.

□ (A) I prefer spending time indoors with family or friends on the weekend.

□ (B) I prefer spending time outdoors with family or friends on the weekend.

Because ....

....

2. Make a group with two or three partners who have the same preference and present your thoughts. Write down the important key words in each box while listening to others.

Key words: Group member 1	Key words: Group member 2	Key words: Group member 3

3. Using your group member's key words, form one collective opinion.

....

....

....

4. Present your group's opinion to the class.

Unit 8

The United States: A Nation on the Road

自動車大国、アメリカとは！

Pre-Reading Activity

Look at picture 1. Guess what the white truck is doing. Talk to your partner in English.

Vocabulary Map

Use the words in the box to complete the vocabulary map.

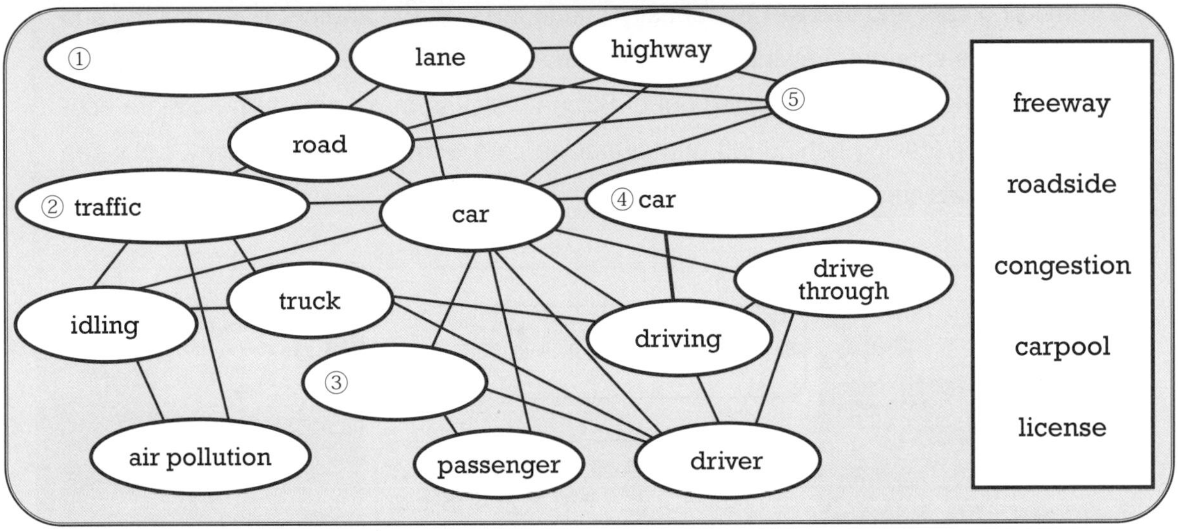

Reading

23

Americans love their cars. No car means no getting anywhere in the United States. In many states, you can apply for a car license when you turn 16. This is one of the reasons why you will often see high school students driving to school. Some freeways have six lanes, and there are many roadside hotels called “motels,” typically with parking directly outside. Having a car is something that is absolutely necessary for daily American life.

Did you know the drive-through system was created in America? Nowadays, you are able to do a lot of chores without getting out of the car. There are drive-through ATMs, dry cleaners, and pharmacies to pick up medication. What is more, there are even drive-through funeral halls and wedding chapels! Drive-throughs work very well for the car-centric culture of the U.S.

This car culture has even been extended to garbage trucks. The truck driver can empty a garbage can at the curb without leaving the truck. That is because the truck has large robotic arms that do all the work. More specifically, the arms extend out from the truck and grab the trash can; then the arms shake the can and empty the trash into a large collection container. Thanks to America’s wide roads, these trucks are quite common.

Having a lot of cars in a country may sound harmful to the environment. However, there have been many efforts put in place to reduce carbon emissions in the U.S. For instance, in bigger cities, there is a High Occupancy Vehicle (HOV) lane, aka a carpool lane, which typically has a big diamond mark on it. This restricts the minimum number of passengers in a car to two people and cuts down the number of cars on the highway in order to decrease traffic congestion and air pollution.

However, there have been some changes to America’s car culture. For example, some communities across the U.S. have started to ban the construction of drive-through lanes in newer fast-food restaurants. This is to help reduce the emissions from idling cars and to lower the obesity rate in the U.S. On another note, electric and autonomous cars are drawing more attention. Therefore, more car manufacturers are relying on the technology coming out of Silicon Valley to make smarter and more eco-friendly cars, leaving behind old and oversized cars with bad fuel economy. Let’s see how America’s car culture continues to evolve in the future.

(406 words)

薬局のドライブスルーに並ぶ車

HOV（相乗り車専用）のレーンと、それを示す路上のダイヤモンドマーク

Find the following words in a dictionary and write their meanings in the parentheses below. Fill in the bracket with an appropriate word to complete the phrase.

Words and Phrases ★予習しておこう！

car license	自動車運転免許証	carpool	( )
freeway	（米の）高速道路	restrict	制限する
roadside	道路沿いの	minimum	最少の
chore	（家事などの）雑用	highway	幹線道路
pharmacy	薬局	congestion	( )
funeral	葬式	air pollution	大気（空気）汚染
car-centric	車中心の	ban	禁じる
extend	広がる、伸びる	idling	アイドリング
empty	空にする	obesity	肥満
curb	( )	on another note	もうひとつ言うなら
more specifically	より具体的に言えば	autonomous	自動の
collection container	収集用コンテナ	draw attention	注目を集める
thanks to ~	～のおかげで	manufacturer	製造会社
harmful	( )	rely [ ] ~	～を頼りにする
carbon emissions	炭素排出量	eco-friendly	( )
aka	別名	oversized	大きすぎる

Reading Exercises

A *You will hear three questions about the passage. Select the best answer and circle (A), (B) or (C).* 24

1. What is a new trend in the U.S.?
   (A) People visit fast-food restaurants more often.
   (B) Companies are getting more interested in electric cars.
   (C) More students prefer drive-through pharmacies.

2.
   (A) They can run
   (B) They can collect
   (C) They can empty

3.
   (A)
   (B)
   (C)

B *Circle the best choice to complete the following sentences.*

1.You can apply _____ a car license when you turn 16.

(A) in
(B) with
(C) for
(D) under

2. You are able to do a lot of _____ without getting out of the car.

(A) chores
(B) packages
(C) avenues
(D) handles

3. _____ specifically, the arms extend out from the truck and grab the trash can.

(A) Many
(B) Better
(C) Least
(D) More

4. There have been many efforts _____ to reduce carbon emissions in the U.S.

(A) put in place
(B) pull over place
(C) peak to place
(D) punch back place

C *Based on the information in the passage, write "T" if it is true, or "F" if it is false.*

1. You can get a car license at a younger age in the U.S. than in Japan. (   )
2. One purpose of a carpool lane is to reduce carbon emissions. (   )
3. More and more big cars will be driven in the U.S. in the future. (   )

D *Rearrange the words and phrases in the (   ) to complete the sentences.*

1. 電動自動車や無人自動車がより多くの注目を浴びている。

Electric and (attention / cars / drawing / autonomous / more / are) .

Electric and (____

____).

2. より多くの車製造会社がシリコンバレーで生まれた科学技術に頼っている。

More car (the / on / manufacturers / technology / coming / relying / are) out of Silicon Valley.

More car (____

____) out of Silicon Valley.

Conversation

Listen to the conversation and answer the following. For ① and ③, fill in the blanks. For ②, choose the right words. For ④, put the words in the { } in the right order.

Kenta: You know, I've been ① (   ) (   ) the difference between Japanese gratin and American macaroni and cheese. I've seen mac and cheese in a TV series a lot and thought it was gratin.

Paul: Yeah, they look almost the same, but Japanese gratin is usually baked and topped with cheese, while mac and cheese is a mix of macaroni and a creamy cheese sauce.

Nancy: Traditionally, it was baked in the oven, but it's not necessary. In fact, you can buy instant mac and cheese products everywhere. There are ② { fronted and backed / flies and bugs / frozen and boxed } ones.

Paul: Yeah, all you have to do is cook the macaroni and mix in some powdered cheese sauce.

Kenta: So simple! It's like Japanese instant ramen.

Nancy: Exactly. You can add meat or vegetables if you like, but mostly I eat it just as is.

Kenta: ③ (   ) (   ), but I think Americans eat too much unhealthy food.

Paul: Well, it depends. I think you got a point because ④ ({ plenty / true / it's / that / of / there's } → ____________________________________) people who eat junk food like pizza and burgers on a daily basis. However, we also have a lot of vegans in the States.

Kenta: Vegans? Don't you mean vegetarians?

Nancy: No, vegans don't eat any animal products, including eggs, dairy products, and even honey.

Choose the picture that does not match the conversation and circle the number.

(1)

(2)

(3)

(4)

Column

文化を知るための Language：英語 (English)

The squeaky wheel gets the grease.

車社会のアメリカでは、車に関する様々な興味深い表現があります。たとえば上のことわざは、直訳は「キーキー鳴る車輪は油をさされる」ですが、その意味は「きちんと意見を述べれば、その見返りがある」です。思うことはきちんと声をだして主張すべき、というアメリカ人の考えをうまく映し出しています。日本には「沈黙は金 (*Silence is golden.*)」という、静かでいることをよしとする教訓がありますが、互いに逆を指しており面白いですね。

車関連の表現には、日本語と英語で異なる単語を使うべきものが多くあります。たとえば、運転席の「ハンドル」は英語では *(steering) wheel* 、「パンクタイヤ」は *flat tire* と言うのが一般的です。また日本で「マフラー」といえば首に巻く防寒着ですが、アメリカで *muffler* といえば主に「排気ガスが出る管」になります。また英米語の違いもあり、ボンネット (*bonnet*) は英国語的で、米国語ではよく *hood* が使われます。身近な乗り物だからこそ、ことばが独自の進化を遂げているようです。

Group Presentation

1. Which do you prefer, (A) or (B)? Put a check mark (✓) and write your reason in the box.

☐ (A) I prefer living in a place where I have to drive everywhere.

☐ (B) I prefer living in a place where I have to take public transportation everywhere.

➡ Because ……………………………………………………………………………

……………………………………………………………………………………………

2. Make a group with two or three partners who have the same preference and present your thoughts. Write down the important key words in each box while listening to others.

Key words: Group member 1	Key words: Group member 2	Key words: Group member 3

3. Using your group member's key words, form one collective opinion.

……………………………………………………………………………………………

……………………………………………………………………………………………

……………………………………………………………………………………………

4. Present your group's opinion to the class.

Unit 9

France: A Place of Little Waste

効率重視のフランス文化とは！

Pre-Reading Activity

Look at picture 1. Guess what the item is. Talk to your partner in English.

Vocabulary Map

Use the words in the box to complete the vocabulary map.

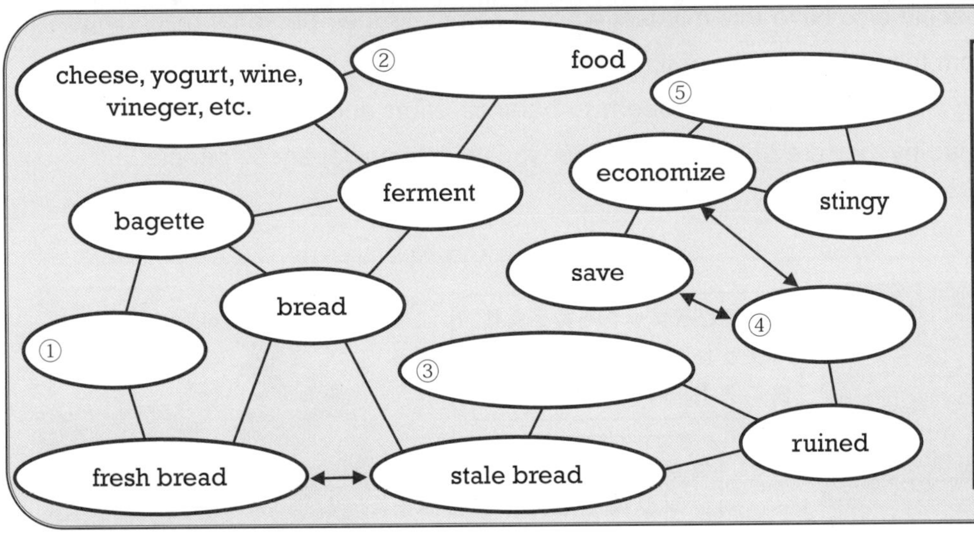

bakery
cheapskate
waste
leftover
fermented

Reading

When we think of France, we often think of bread and wine. Wine is an important part of family meals or dinner with friends. On weekend mornings, you can see many people buying freshly made baguettes at their favorite bakeries. And no matter how much bread or wine the French enjoy, they never waste any of it.

In Japan, French toast is a very popular food that you can enjoy in cafes and first-class hotels. In France, it is called *pain perdu,* which literally means “ruined bread.” It is traditionally made with leftover, stale bread. Fresh bread is never used to make it. After all, why waste a fresh baguette to make “ruined bread”?

Not only will the French try not to waste bread, they will use up every drop of wine. Leftover wine is added into a *vinaigrier*, a pot used to make vinegar. Once the wine ferments into vinegar, they can use it for cooking. But not everyone chooses to use up their wine this way. Young people, especially, will drink it all up without wasting a drop.

A common stereotype about the French is that they are cheapskates. Is that true? Of course, there are people who fit the stereotype and those who do not. However, most French people tend not to like wasting things. From the Japanese point of view, this could be seen as being stingy or even lazy.

For example, in a French kitchen, you will find a *torchon*, which is a kitchen towel. *Torchons* are used to wipe many things in the kitchen: dishes, tables, countertops, and even hands. The French do not keep separate towels for these things. They just use a *torchon*. Using one cloth to wipe everything in the kitchen could be seen as lazy, but they often think, “What’s wrong with using one towel to dry dishes and wipe our hands? Our hands are clean after washing the dishes!” Also, kitchen sponges are used to clean tables as well as the dishes! A lot of Japanese would be shocked to see someone clean their tables with their dishwashing sponge.

French people also have this mindset when it comes to their personal belongings. Many of them think it is a waste of time to work extra hours to buy a new thing when an old thing works just fine. They seem to balance effort and efficiency quite well. Maybe this is why they are able to take longer vacations than Japanese people.

(412 words)

パン屋でバゲットを買う女性。バゲットは半分むき出しの紙袋に入れられるのが一般的

食器スポンジでキッチンシンク周りを掃除する様子

Find the following words in a dictionary and write their meanings in the parentheses below. Fill in the bracket with an appropriate word to complete the phrase.

Words and Phrases			★ 予習しておこう！
freshly made	作りたての	ferment	発酵する
baguette	バゲット（フランスパン）	drink ~ all [ ]	～を全て飲み干す
bakery	パン屋	stereotype	固定概念
waste	( )	cheapskate	( )
literally	文字通りに	fit	一致する、適合する
ruined	だめになった	tend to do ~	～する傾向がある
traditionally	従来（伝統的に）	point of view	視点、観点
leftover	( )	stingy	( )
stale	（パン等が）硬くなった	wipe	拭く
dish	皿、料理	countertop	調理台
use up	使い切る	mindset	（個人の）考え方
drop	一滴	when it comes to ~	～に関して言えば
add	加える	personal belongings	（個人の）持ち物
pot	（陶器の）つぼ	balance A and B	AとBのつり合いを取る
vinegar	酢	efficiency	( )

Reading Exercises

A *You will hear three questions about the passage. Select the best answer and circle (A), (B) or (C).* 27

1. Why is a *torchon* special?
   (A) It is used to wipe different kinds of things in the kitchen.
   (B) It is a kitchen towel made of colorful sponge.
   (C) It is too clean for Japanese people to use.

2.
   (A) The way
   (B) The way
   (C) The way

3.
   (A)
   (B)
   (C)

B *Circle the best choice to complete the following sentences.*

1. People in France do not _____ fresh bread to make French toast.

(A) add
(B) waste
(C) wash
(D) ruined

2. _____ the French try not to waste bread, they will use up every drop of wine.

(A) Not only will
(B) Only will not
(C) Will only not
(D) Will not only

3. _____ with using one towel to dry dishes and wipe our hands?

(A) Aren't you
(B) How come
(C) What if
(D) What's wrong

4. Many French people think it is a waste of time _____ extra hours to buy a new thing.

(A) works
(B) to work
(C) being worked
(D) have worked

C *Based on the information in the passage, write "T" if it is true, or "F" if it is false.*

1. French people think that French toast is a special food served at special occasions. (　　)
2. Some people traditionally think that people in France are cheapskates. (　　)
3. Japanese people would be surprised to see that French people do not clean tables. (　　)

D *Rearrange the words and phrases in the (　) to complete the sentences.*

1. フランス人はいかに多くのパンやワインを満喫しようとも、無駄にすることは絶対にない。
(how / no / the French / bread or wine / much /matter) enjoy, they never waste any of it.
(____
____________________________) enjoy, they never waste any of it.

2. 日本人の目から見れば、このことはケチというか、むしろ怠惰であるとみなされるかもしれない。
From the Japanese point of view, (could / as / stingy / be / being / this / or / seen) even lazy.
From the Japanese point of view, (______________________________
____) even lazy.

Conversation

Listen to the conversation and answer the following. For ①, choose the right words. For ②, put the words in the { } in the right order. For ③ and ④, fill in the blanks. 28

Kenta: What is this? Is it like a *takoyaki* maker or something?

Francoise: Nice guess! It's an escargot dish. I bought it when I went back to France.

Kenta: Oh, escargot! I've ① { heard of / heard at / hard at } it. What is it exactly?

Mathieu: It's snail.

Kenta: Ew! That's gross! Do you guys eat snails?

Mathieu: Ah, yes and no. Actually, I'm ② ({ big / of / not / fan / a } → ______________ ______________________________) escargot. I don't like the texture.

Francoise: Come on! They are delicious! And Kenta, no offence, but you people eat eel. That's gross.

Kenta: What's ③ (   ) (   ) eel? You're just judging it by its appearance.

Mathieu: Speaking of weird foods, I don't eat frog legs, either.

Kenta: Ah, I saw an American describing French people in movies as "frogs."

Francoise: That's a typical insult used to refer to French people, but I don't think the French eat frog legs that often.

Mathieu: ④ (   ) (   ) how Japanese people don't eat sea urchin or salmon roe every day.

Choose the picture that does not match the conversation and circle the number.

(1)

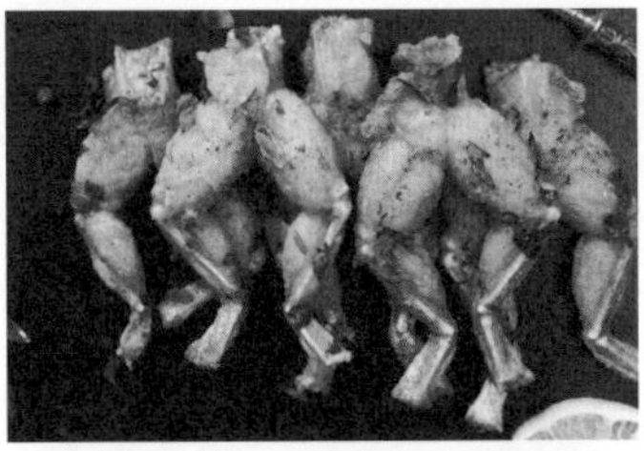

(2)

(3)

(4)

Column

文化を知るための Language：フランス語 (Français)

***C'est gentil.*「セ・ジャンティ」**

フランス人はほめられたときに、どのように返すと思いますか。欧米では、ほめことばをダイレクトに受け止めて、相手に感謝の意を述べることが多いと思われますが、フランス人にも *Merci.*（ありがとう）とお礼を言う人が多いです。日本人はほめられると、「とんでもない」や「いえ、全然」などのように、自分に向けられたほめことばを否定して謙遜する人が多いですが、フランス人にはこのような習慣はありません。

Merci 以外で、フランス人がほめられたときによく使っている表現に、*C'est gentil.*（ご親切に）というものがあります。日本人が相手のほめことばを否定して謙遜するのに対して、フランス人は *C'est gentil.* という返しで相手のほめことばを否定も肯定もせず、ほめてくれる相手のやさしさについて言及することで、尊大な印象にならないようにしているのかもしれません。

Group Presentation

1. Which do you prefer, (A) or (B)? Put a check mark (✓) and write your reason in the box.

☐ (A) I want to earn more money by giving up my life to work.

☐ (B) I want to keep my life as is and work as little as possible.

Because ....

....

2. Make a group with two or three partners who have the same preference and present your thoughts. Write down the important key words in each box while listening to others.

Key words: Group member 1	Key words: Group member 2	Key words: Group member 3

3. Using your group member's key words, form one collective opinion.

....

....

....

4. Present your group's opinion to the class.

Unit 10

Bangladesh: Where Chaos and Peace Coexist

バングラデシュの混沌とのどかさとは！

Pre-Reading Activity

Look at picture 1. Guess what patterns do you see on the fabric. Talk to your partner in English.

1

2

3

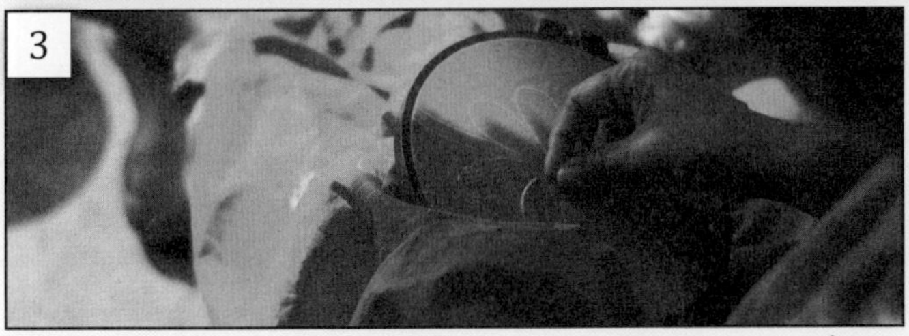

4

Vocabulary Map

Use the words in the box to complete the vocabulary map.

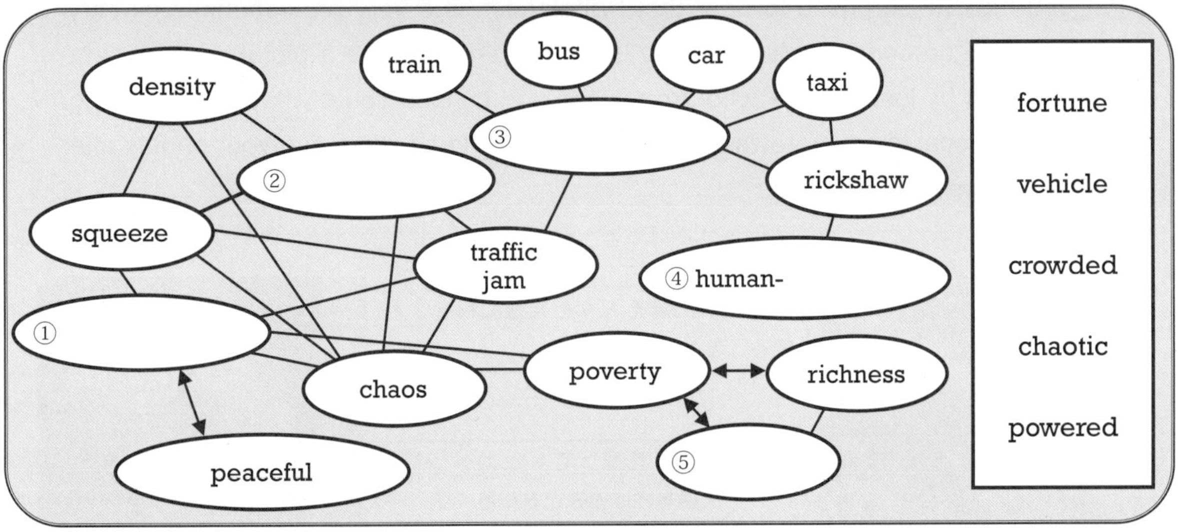

Reading

29

In Bangladesh, you may encounter chaotic situations in daily life. Tourists, especially, may be astonished by the heavy traffic jams. Dhaka, the capital and largest city in Bangladesh, has a large population density. The bus terminals and train stations are so crowded with people and the streets with cars that you cannot tell what is going on. The way the locals take buses and trains can also be very shocking. It seems as if they don't have a concept of safe riding capacity, as they try to squeeze as many people into a vehicle as possible. Some even sit on the roof of a bus or a train. You can also see a jumble of green-colored, three-wheeled vehicles called *CNG* and human-powered taxis called rickshaws on the road.

Some people imagine Bangladesh to be a country full of chaos, poverty, and flooding. However, away from cities like Dhaka, you will be surprised at how peaceful it is. These peaceful places are reflected on a type of embroidered quilt called a *nakshi katha*. *Nakshi* means "design," and *katha* means "cloth" in Bengali, the language of Bangladesh. The quilt has unique and interesting patterns embroidered onto it, such as children playing, animals, lotus flowers, houses and so on. Also, each design has a meaning, such as an elephant being a symbol of fortune. *Nakshi katha* are used to make couch cushion covers, tapestries, etc., and they are popular items abroad.

Bangladesh is strongly influenced by Islam, and a lot of people used to think that women should stay at home. But nowadays, women in bigger cities are participating in society more than ever. However, women in rural areas don't have enough opportunities to get an education. Therefore, it is difficult for them to find work. Under these circumstances, making homemade *nakshi katha* has become an important way for these women to support themselves. Traditionally, *nakshi katha* are passed down from mother to daughter, and the embroideries express daily life from a woman's point of view.

You may be surprised to hear that Bangladesh is a very pro-Japanese country, so you will be comfortable traveling there. When you take a picture, you will be surrounded by local people who are smiling and curious about what you are doing. It's not unusual to have grown-ups and children try to squeeze into your photos after staying there for a few days.

(396 words)

駅で汽車に乗る人々と乗客に物を売る行商人たち

「写真を撮って」とカメラに笑顔を向ける子どもたち

Find the following words in a dictionary and write their meanings in the parentheses below. Fill in the bracket with an appropriate word to complete the phrase.

Words and Phrases ★ 予習しておこう！

encounter	出くわす	flooding	洪水
chaotic	混沌とした	peaceful	(　　　　　　　)
be astonished by ~	～に仰天する	be reflected on ~	～に反映する
traffic jam	交通渋滞	embroidered	刺しゅう入りの
population density	(　　　　　　　)	fortune	富、財産
be crowded with ~	～で混雑する	be influenced by ~	～に影響を受ける
the locals	地元の住民	participate [　　　] ~	～に参加する
riding capacity	乗車定員	rural area	農村地域、田舎
squeeze … into ~	～に…を押し込む	under these circumstances	このような状況で
vehicle	乗り物	embroidery	(　　　　　　　)
jumble	ごちゃ混ぜ	point of view	視点、観点
human-powered	人力による	pro-Japanese	親日家の
rickshaw	人力車、リクシャ	be surrounded by ~	～に囲まれる
chaos	(　　　　　　　)	be curious about ~	～に好奇心を持つ
poverty	(　　　　　　　)	squeeze into ~	～に無理に押し入る

Reading Exercises

A *You will hear three questions about the passage. Select the best answer and circle (A), (B) or (C).* 30

1. What is a recent change to women's lives in Bangladesh?
   (A) They have less chance to have a good education.
   (B) They are participating more in society.
   (C) They make many more *nakshi katha* than before.

2.
   (A) Very crowded
   (B) Human-powered
   (C) A language

3.
   (A)
   (B)
   (C)

B *Circle the best choice to complete the following sentences.*

1. Dhaka has a _____ population density.

(A) many
(B) giant
(C) large
(D) wide

2. It seems _____ they don't have a concept of safe riding capacity.

(A) as to
(B) as if
(C) what if
(D) if not

3. These peaceful places are reflected _____ a type of embroidered quilt called a *nakshi katha.*

(A) above
(B) into
(C) forward
(D) on

4. The embroideries express daily life from a woman's _____.

(A) point of view
(B) point of no return
(C) point of agreement
(D) point of action

C *Based on the information in the passage, write "T" if it is true, or "F" if it is false.*

1. Bangladesh is known as one of the richest countries in the world. (　　)
2. There are a lot of Muslims in Bangladesh. (　　)
3. Japanese travelers seem to be welcomed in Bangladesh. (　　)

D *Rearrange the words and phrases in the (　) to complete the sentences.*

1. 伝統的に、ノクシカタは母から娘へと受け継がれます。
Traditionally, *nakshi katha* (daughter / down / are / mother / to / passed / from).
Traditionally, *nakshi katha* (______________________________
______________________________).

2. 大人や子供があなたの写真に写り込もうとすることも珍しくはありません。
It's not unusual to have grown-ups and children (photos / to / into / squeeze / your / try).
It's not unusual to have grown-ups and children (______________________________
______________________________).

Conversation

Listen to the conversation and answer the following. For ①, choose the right words. For ②, put the words in the { } in the right order. For ③ and ④, fill in the blanks. 31

Kenta: A friend of mine said he was very surprised when someone who he just met invited him ① { off and all / over for / on forward } dinner in Bangladesh. Does that happen a lot?

Tariq: Ah, yeah. That's *dawat*, which is a Bengali word meaning "invitation to a feast." It is so common to invite people over for meals that we have a word for it.

Barsha: Yes, especially if you are a foreigner. They may be more curious to talk to you and want to be kind to you. So it is quite possible to get a dinner invitation ② ({ chat / having/ little / even / a / after } → ______________________ ____).

Kenta: Wow, I would feel awkward to have dinner at a near-stranger's home.

Tariq: Also, if you get a dinner invitation, you cannot leave until you finish your meal.

Kenta: Wow, I see. What kind of food do you have for *dawat*?

Barsha: We serve *torkari*, which is what you'd call curry. You can have many kinds of *torkaris* such as fish, vegetable, egg and so on.

Tariq: And you are ③ (   ) (   ) eat with your right hand.

Kenta: Really? Do you have to eat with your hand?

Barsha: Yes. You mix your rice and *torkari* well with your hand and ④ (   ) them (   ) into your mouth. In that way, you can enjoy your food much more than eating with a spoon.

Choose the picture that does not match the conversation and circle the number.

(1)

(2)

(3)

(4)

Column

文化を知るためのLanguage：ベンガル語（বাঙালি）

সমস্যা নেই「ショモッシャナイ」

バングラデシュでは、誰かに何かを頼むときに大丈夫かどうかを聞くと、すぐに「ショモッシャナイ（問題ない）」という答えが返ってきます。しかし、実際に問題なくスムーズに事が運ぶことはあまりないかもしれません。

タクシーの運転手に行き先を告げたとき「ショモッシャナイ」と言われても、迷わず目的地にたどり着くとは限りません。しかし、バングラデシュでは、運転手が道を聞きながらでも最終的に到達すればショモッシャナイですし、電車やバスが時間通りに来なくてもショモッシャナイです。

おおらかなバングラデシュ人にはタクシー運転手が行き先を知らないことや電車やバスが 1、2 時間遅れることは細かいことなのです。ただ、公共交通機関の運行は 1 分単位で正確であることが当たり前、タクシーの運転手は常に最短ルートで走ってくれて当然、と思っている日本人には、バングラデシュでの「ショモッシャナイ」状況は「全然ショモッシャナイじゃない！」かもしれません。

Group Presentation

1. Which do you prefer, (A) or (B)? Put a check mark (✓) and write your reason in the box.

☐ (A) A society where buses, trains, and people, including you, are punctual.

☐ (B) A society where buses, trains, and people, including you, do not have to be punctual.

➡ Because ....

....

2. Make a group with two or three partners who have the same preference and present your thoughts. Write down the important key words in each box while listening to others.

Key words: Group member 1	Key words: Group member 2	Key words: Group member 3

3. Using your group member's key words, form one collective opinion.

....

....

....

4. Present your group's opinion to the class.

Unit 11

New Zealand: Where Native Culture Thrives

共生のニュージーランド文化とは！

Pre-Reading Activity

Look at picture 2. Guess what the item is. Talk to your partner in English.

1

2

3

4

Vocabulary Map

Use the words in the box to complete the vocabulary map.

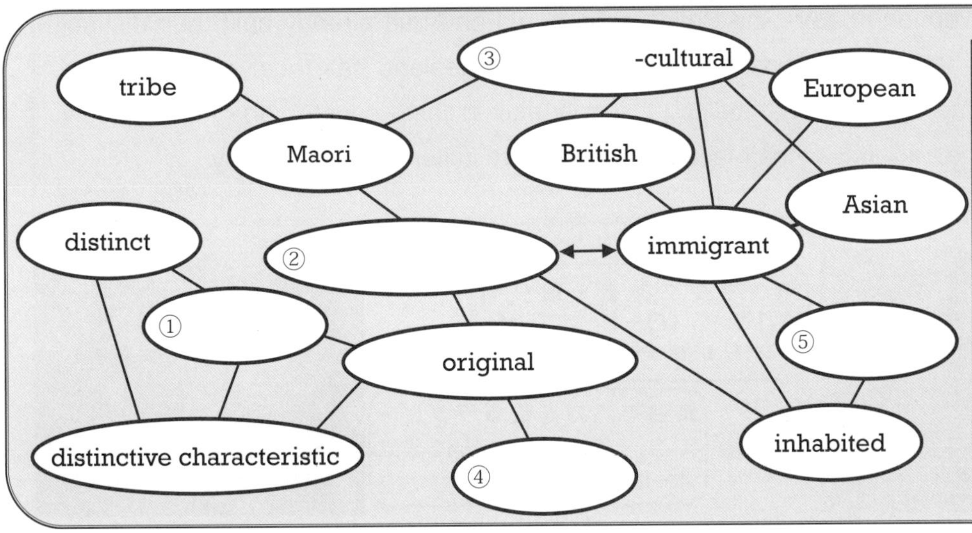

unique

multi

settler

originally

indigenous

Reading

When Japanese people think about New Zealand, many of them picture an island that is close to Australia, filled with a bunch of sheep. Actually, the number of sheep on the island is several times more than the population of people there. You may also think of the film series, *The Lord of the Rings*, as New Zealand was the filming location for these movies.

Speaking of New Zealand, woolen products or products that look like sheep might also come to mind. However, there is another thing that the country is famous for around the world: "manuka honey." This popular souvenir is also known as "miracle honey" because of its antibacterial effects. The honey has been drawing attention from all over the world. Manuka honey is a traditional product that is made from flowers called "manuka." Manuka flowers only grow in certain places in New Zealand. The indigenous people of New Zealand, known as the Maori, have used the honey as a medicine since ancient times. They eat it when they have a sore throat or use it to treat wounds.

You may not have heard the word "Maori," but you probably have heard of a very successful rugby team called "The All Blacks." The All Blacks are New Zealand's international male rugby team. They are one of the strongest rugby teams in the world, often occupying the number one spot even before the introduction of the World Rugby Rankings in 2003. They perform a traditional Maori dance before their matches called a "haka dance." It has become a distinctive characteristic of the team.

The haka is a type of ancient Maori war dance traditionally used on the battlefield. The haka fiercely displays a tribe's pride, strength and unity. The dance includes violent foot-stomping, sticking out of the tongue, and rhythmic body slapping. Nowadays, haka are still performed during Maori ceremonies to honor guests and at weddings. Most students in New Zealand learn how to do the haka at school, even though they may not have a Maori background.

You may think New Zealand was originally inhabited by Europeans. In fact, the Maori people arrived long before the British settlers did and had already built their distinct culture with its rich traditions. More recently, New Zealand has received immigrants from Asia and other nations, making it a truly multi-cultural country; one that uniquely combines the traditions of the Maori and the modern culture we know today.

(406 words)

マタマタにある一般公開されている『ロード・オブ・ザ・リング』のセット

試合でハカを踊るラグビーニュージーランド代表のオールブラックス

Find the following words in a dictionary and write their meanings in the parentheses below. Fill in the bracket with an appropriate word to complete the phrase.

Words and Phrases ★ 予習しておこう！

be filled with ~	〜で一杯になる	battlefield	戦場
a bunch of ~	たくさんの	fiercely	激しく
~ times more	〜倍以上	display	（感情を）表す
filming location	撮影場所	tribe	(　　　　　)
woolen	羊毛の	unity	結束
come to mind	思い浮かぶ	foot-stomping	足踏み
souvenir	（旅行の）お土産	stick out	突き出る
be known [　　　] ~	〜と知られて	slapping	平手打ち
antibacterial effect	抗菌作用	honor guests	来賓を迎える
draw attention	話題を呼ぶ	originally	そもそも、もともと
indigenous	(　　　　　)	inhabit	居住する
ancient times	古代、大昔	settler	移住者
sore throat	のどの痛み	immigrant	(　　　　　)
treat wounds	傷の手当てをする	multi-cultural	(　　　　　)
occupy	占める	uniquely	(　　　　　)
distinctive characteristic	際立った特徴	combine A and B	A と B を結びつける

Reading Exercises

A *You will hear three questions about the passage. Select the best answer and circle (A), (B) or (C).* 33

1. How are New Zealand and *The Lord of the Rings* films related to each other?
   (A) The film was a big success in New Zealand.
   (B) People in New Zealand got very upset when they saw the movie.
   (C) Many parts of the movies were filmed in New Zealand.

2.
   (A) Their wool
   (B) Their wool
   (C) Their wool

3.
   (A)
   (B)
   (C)

B *Circle the best choice to complete the following sentences.*

1. There is another thing that New Zealand is famous _____ around the world.

(A) in
(B) to
(C) of
(D) for

2. The All Blacks are a strong rugby team and often _____ the number one spot.

(A) crush
(B) occupy
(C) figure
(D) disclose

3. The haka dance has become a _____ characteristic of the All Blacks.

(A) differ
(B) differentiate
(C) distinctive
(D) disappoint

4. The haka is a type of ancient Maori war dance _____ used on the battlefield.

(A) trade
(B) tradition
(C) traditional
(D) traditionally

C *Based on the information in the passage, write "T" if it is true, or "F" if it is false.*

1. The Maori people have recently started using manuka honey as a medicine. (　　)
2. The All Blacks perform a haka dance every time their match ends. (　　)
3. Maori people had already arrived in New Zealand when the British settlers came there. (　　)

D *Rearrange the words and phrases in the (　) to complete the sentences.*

1. 島にいる羊の数は、人口の数倍に及ぶ。
The number of sheep on the island (several / times / more / than / the / is / population) of people there.
The number of sheep on the island (______________________________
______________________________) of people there.

2. ニュージーランドは他国からの移民を受け入れており、それがこの国を真の多文化国家にしている。
NZ has received immigrants from other nations, (a truly / multi-cultural / it / country / making).
NZ has received immigrants from other nations, (______________________________
______________________________).

Conversation

Listen to the conversation and answer the following. For ①, put the words in the { } in the right order. For ② and ④, fill in the blanks. For ③, choose the right words. 34

Kenta: Can I have butter or something for my toast?

Nikau: Sure. Ah, yes, you might want to try Marmite. My mother ①({ from / sent / it / me / to } → ______________________________) New Zealand.

Sarah: Great! I missed it so much!

Kenta: What's that again? It looks like chocolate spread.

Sarah: Marmite. It's a ② ( ) spread for bread and crackers. Try some! It might smell a bit strange.

Kenta: Oh, yuck! It smells ... original... Sorry, I'll pass.

Nikau: OK. I've got kiwifruit jam. ③ { He you all / Hear you up / Here you are }.

Kenta: Thanks. This looks good! Kiwifruit is quite common in Japan, but the jam is rare.

Sarah: It's everywhere in New Zealand. We often eat it with cereal or yogurt.

Kenta: Don't you have a bird called a kiwi in New Zealand? The one which cannot fly.

Nikau: Yes. Actually, the kiwifruit was ④ ( ) ( ) the kiwi bird. I heard the fruit was originally from China.

Sarah: No way! Are you sure? I thought the kiwifruit was native to New Zealand!

Choose the picture that does not match the conversation and circle the number.

(1)

(2)

(3)

(4)

Column

文化を知るための Language：ニュージーランド英語等 (NZ English, etc.)

Kiwi

ニュージーランドには、ほとんどの国民が使っている英語、先住民マオリ族のマオリ語、そして、ニュージーランド手話の３つの公用語があります。ニュージーランドは世界で初めて手話が公用語になった国です。この手話はイギリス手話が基になっていて、マオリ語のことばのコンセプトも取り入れられています。

ニュージーランドの英語は *Kiwi English* とも呼ばれ、イギリス英語が基盤になっています。*Kiwi* は名詞で「ニュージーランド人」、また「ニュージーランドらしい」という意味でも使われますが、差別的なニュアンスはなく、現地の人にも愛着を持って使われています。*Kiwi English* にはマオリ語からの借用語もたくさんあります。実は、*Kiwi* という語もマオリ語から来たことばだそうです。

イギリスからの移民の言語、先住民の言語、手話という全く異なる３つのことばが公用語になっているという点からも、ニュージーランドは人々が共生できる社会を目指していることが伺えます。

Group Presentation

1. Which do you prefer, (A) or (B)? Put a check mark (✓) and write your reason in the box.

☐ (A) If I move to a different country, I would adapt to the culture or customs.

☐ (B) If I move to a different country, I would keep Japanese traditions and customs.

➡ Because ....

....

2. Make a group with two or three partners who have the same preference and present your thoughts. Write down the important key words in each box while listening to others.

Key words: Group member 1	Key words: Group member 2	Key words: Group member 3

3. Using your group member's key words, form one collective opinion.

....

....

....

4. Present your group's opinion to the class.

Unit 12

South Korea: The Crossroads of Food, Culture, and Tradition

食で深まるきずな文化とは！

Pre-Reading Activity

Look at picture 1. Guess what the item is. Talk to your partner in English.

Vocabulary Map

Use the words in the box to complete the vocabulary map.

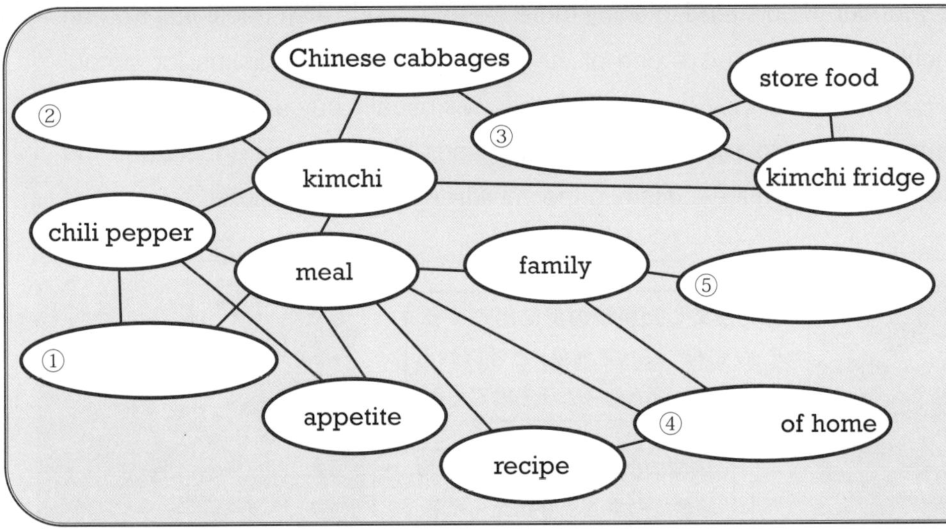

household

refrigerator

seasoning

taste

fermentation

Reading

35

Did you know there are over 300 kinds of kimchi in Korea? Kimchi is eaten as is, but it is also a must-have seasoning in the kitchen. In the early days, kimchi did not contain chili pepper at all. When chili peppers came to Korea, people used to put it in their boots to keep out the cold in winter. Afterwards, it is said that they started to put chili pepper in food to increase appetite.

Every year, all members of the family gather for an event called *Gimjang*. It is one of the biggest events in Korea, and it is dedicated to kimchi making. During this event, the art of kimchi making is passed down from parent to child. Each family has their own style and recipe for making kimchi, so this is a good time for them to teach their children and grandchildren their family recipe. Everyone will work together to make enough kimchi for one year. Not only is this a good family-bonding event, but it is also a good community-building event.

There is a big announcement in Korea called the *Gimjang jeonseon* front. This is the time of year when the weather is perfect for kimchi making. On each day leading up to the *Gimjang* event, the lowest temperature should be zero degrees Celsius, and the average temperature should be less than four. The *Gimjang jeonseon* front comes down from the north to the south of Korea. Korean people refer to the *jeonseon* and decide on when they can make the best kimchi.

During *Gimjang*, 100 to 200 Chinese cabbages are used to make kimchi. But how can they store so much kimchi at home? Every Korean household has two refrigerators: a regular refrigerator and a kimchi refrigerator. These kimchi fridges are specially designed to store kimchi at the perfect temperature for fermentation. They are also large enough to store one year's worth of kimchi made during *Gimjang*. There is also a special filter built in that stops the smell of the kimchi from escaping.

These days, younger people tend to enjoy more western foods than traditional Korean foods like kimchi, even though it is one of the most common side dishes for school lunch meals. However, once they get married, they will usually buy a kimchi fridge just like their parents and grandparents did. These traditions let them truly understand the taste of home and pass down the custom to their children and grandchildren.

(409 words)

店で注文した料理の前に出てくる
ミッパンチャン(常備菜)と呼ばれる
小皿料理。いろんなキムチも出てくる

韓国の小学校のある日の給食。
給食にもキムチが添えられる

Find the following words in a dictionary and write their meanings in the parentheses below. Fill in the bracket with an appropriate word to complete the phrase.

Words and Phrases ★ 予習しておこう！

must-have	なくてはならない	average	平均の
seasoning	(　　　　　　　　)	refer to ~	～を参照する
contain	含む、入れている	Chinese cabbage	白菜
chili pepper	唐辛子	store	貯蔵する、たくわえる
keep out	侵入を防ぐ	household	世帯、家族
increase	増進させる、増やす	refrigerator (fridge)	(　　　　　　　　)
appetite	(　　　　　　　　)	regular	通常の、いつもの
gather for ~	～のために集まる	fermentation	(　　　　　　　　)
be dedicated [　　　] ~	～に専念する	... worth of ~	…分（相当）の～
recipe	調理法、レシピ	escape	漏れる、逃げる
family-bonding	家族のきずな	tend to ~	(　　　　　　　　)
announcement	発表、お知らせ	side dish	付け合わせ、おかず
temperature	気温	taste of home	家庭の味
degree	（温度などの）度	pass down	（次の世代に）伝える
Celsius	摂氏	custom	しきたり、風習

Reading Exercises

A *You will hear three questions about the passage. Select the best answer and circle (A), (B) or (C).* 36

1. What kind of information does *Gimjang jeonseon* front provide?
   (A) The best timing to make kimchi
   (B) The best place to meet family members
   (C) The best temperature for kimchi refrigerators

2.
   (A) They use
   (B) They are
   (C) They have

3.
   (A)
   (B)
   (C)

B *Circle the best choice to complete the following sentences.*

1. Kimchi is a must-have _____ in the kitchen in Korea.

(A) measuring
(B) interesting
(C) reasoning
(D) seasoning

2. Not only is this good for family-bonding, _____ it is also good for community-building.

(A) and
(B) or
(C) but
(D) nor

3. Korean people _____ the *jeonseon* and decide on when they can make the best kimchi.

(A) refer to
(B) look for
(C) stand for
(D) carry out

4. These traditions let people pass down the _____ to their children and grandchildren.

(A) custom
(B) customer
(C) customize
(D) customary

C *Based on the information in the passage, write "T" if it is true, or "F" if it is false.*

1. At first, people in Korea put kimchi in their shoes to keep the inside warm. (　　)
2. At *Gimjang*, people in Korea make kimchi with their family. (　　)
3. More and more young people in Korea are into kimchi than ever. (　　)

D *Rearrange the words and phrases in the (　) to complete the sentences.*

1. 食欲増強のために、唐辛子が食品に入れられ始めたと言われている。
It is said that they started to put (increase / chili / appetite / to / pepper / food / in).
It is said that they started to put (____
____).

2. キムチ冷蔵庫は発酵に最適な温度でキムチを保存することに特化して設計されている。
These kimchi fridges are specially (the perfect / to / designed / kimchi / at / for / store / temperature) fermentation.
These kimchi fridges are specially (____
____) fermentation.

Conversation

Listen to the conversation and answer the following. For ①, put the words in the { } in the right order. For ② and ③, fill in the blanks. For ④, choose the right words. 37

Kenta: Wow, this rice bowl is burning hot! I can barely hold it!

Ji-woo: Hey, you are ① ({ up / hold / not / to / it / supposed } → ____________________ ____________________). It's bad manners in Korea.

Shi-yoon: That's right. And because we don't hold our rice bowl while eating, we can keep them in a special heating machine so that it stays really hot.

Kenta: Wow, I didn't know that. That ② (   ) (   ), when I went to a Korean restaurant, I had Korean BBQ. I had trouble using steel chopsticks because they got pretty hot and slippery. Don't you find them difficult to hold?

Ji-woo: I've been using it since I was little, so I'm kind of ③ (   ) (   ) (   ).

Kenta: Oh? Why are the chopsticks made of steel?

Shi-yoon: It is said that steel chopsticks were made to help the old Korean kings check if their food was poisoned.

Ji-woo: That's right. ④ { See you acted two / Steel reacted to / Seals activated } poisons.

Kenta: How interesting! So the chopsticks were used as a poison detector.

Shi-yoon: Yes! Also, with steel chopsticks, you can feel the temperature of the food better when you eat cold and hot meals.

Choose the picture that does not match the conversation and circle the number.

(1)

(2)

(3)

(4)

Column

文化を知るための Language：コリア語 (한국어)

밥먹었어 ?「パッブ・モゴッソ ?」

キャンパス内で友人を見つけたとき、あなたはなんと声をかけますか？韓国では友人同士のあいさつで「パッブ　モゴッソ？」（ご飯を食べた？）と言うことがあります。韓国人の友人から、1日に何度もこの「パッブ　モゴッソ？」と聞かれて、「なんでそんなに何度もご飯のこと聞くのかな」と思うかもしれません。特に食事へ行こうと誘っているわけではありません。「パッブ　モゴッソ？」は「こんにちは」や「おはようございます」と同じように、ただ人と会ったときに使うだけのあいさつ表現なのです。歴史的に韓国はご飯を満足に食べられなかった時間が長く、友人や近所の人に会うと「ちゃんとご飯を食べることができたか？」とよく尋ねていたようです。そしてその後、このことばが一般的なあいさつ表現になった経緯があるようです。そのような背景を考えるとこの「パッブ　モゴッソ？」は、相手を思いやる愛情のこもったあいさつだということがわかりますね。

Group Presentation

1. Which do you prefer, (A) or (B)? Put a check mark (✓) and write your reason in the box.

☐ (A) I prefer to do traditional activities with my family.

☐ (B) I prefer to do traditional activities with my friends.

Because ....

....

2. Make a group with two or three partners who have the same preference and present your thoughts. Write down the important key words in each box while listening to others.

Key words: Group member 1	Key words: Group member 2	Key words: Group member 3

3. Using your group member's key words, form one collective opinion.

....

....

....

4. Present your group's opinion to the class.

Unit 13

Niger: Friendly Faces in a Dry Land

長い挨拶とおしゃべり好き文化とは！

Pre-Reading Activity

Look at picture 2. Guess what the item is used for. Talk to your partner in English.

Vocabulary Map

Use the words in the box to complete the vocabulary map.

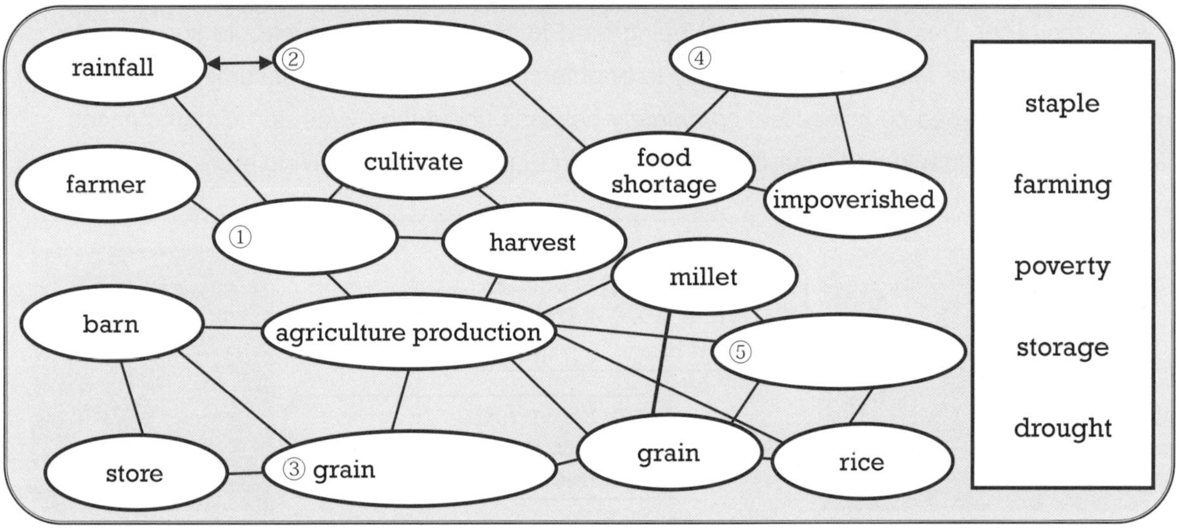

Reading

38

Niger is a country in West Africa. Its population is mostly Muslim. The Sahara Desert occupies most of the land, and most people make their living by farming. Despite the large number of farmers, the land that can be cultivated is only 10 percent. The country is one of the hottest in the world. The temperature can be over 40 degrees Celsius between April and May.

Niger's agricultural production is dependent on rainfall, but because of frequent droughts, the people suffer from food shortages. Therefore, grain is very valuable. In Niger, most farmers keep their harvest at home in a grain storage structure that looks like a small barn made of breathable materials. They grow rice and corn, but millet is their staple food. When they eat, plastic plates as well as dried gourds, or *calabash*, are commonly used. Ceramic tableware is rare.

If you hear about Nigeriens' poverty, you might think that they are saddened and just struggling to live. However, if you think like that, you would be surprised by how they really are. First, you would be impressed with their bright, glittering clothes. They like to wear very colorful and complexly designed clothes, which are for formal situations. People like teachers or civil servants often wear them to work. Second, you would be delighted to see how friendly people are. Nigeriens are usually very chatty.

Nigeriens greet each other warmly. Just saying "Hi" is not enough for them. It is important for them to ask things like, "How's your health?", "Are you OK with the heat?", "How's your work?", "How's your family?" and so on. Once they get to know each other, they like to have a long chit-chat. It is said that it can take two to three times longer to get to your destination because you may be stopped by the locals wanting to talk.

What is more, Nigeriens love having casual powwows with friends. Men do it over tea, and women chat with their neighbors while doing their household chores. By communicating often with people around them, they have a close relationship with each other. Despite entertainment being hard to come by in Niger, people find it fun to communicate with friends and family to brighten their day. We often assume that people in impoverished countries feel completely helpless about their lives and circumstances. However, it may only be our one-sided opinion toward the people living there.

(403 words)

土壁の家が並ぶ村の風景。
農村部には電気や水道もなく、
井戸水を使用

街のひょうたん屋。
乾燥ひょうたんをくりぬいて、
容器や食器として利用

Find the following words in a dictionary and write their meanings in the parentheses below. Fill in the bracket with an appropriate word to complete the phrase.

Words and Phrases ★ 予習しておこう！

desert	砂漠	staple food	(　　　　　)
farming	(　　　　　)	tableware	食器類
cultivate	耕す、栽培する	poverty	貧困
temperature	気温	struggle to ~	必死で～しようとする
agricultural production	農業生産	be impressed with ~	～に感動する
rainfall	降雨、雨量	civil servant	公務員
frequent	頻繁な	chatty	おしゃべり好きな
drought	干ばつ、日照り	greet	(　　　　　)
food shortage	(　　　　　)	the locals	地元の住民
grain	(　　　　　)	chat with ~	～とおしゃべりする
harvest	収穫	household chores	家事
storage	貯蔵庫、保管場所	relationship	人間関係、関係性
barn	納屋	come [　　　]	手に入れる
breathable material	通気性のよい素材	impoverished	貧困に陥った
millet	キビ、アワ、雑穀	circumstances	事情、境遇

Reading Exercises

A *You will hear three questions about the passage. Select the best answer and circle (A), (B) or (C).* 39

1. Which is true about Niger?
   (A) It is rich in natural resources for industry.
   (B) It has multiple rainy seasons in a year.
   (C) It has little in the way of entertainment.

2.
   (A) How
   (B) How
   (C) How

3.
   (A)
   (B)
   (C)

B *Circle the best choice to complete the following sentences.*

1. Niger's agriculture production is _____ on rainfall.

(A) farming
(B) chatty
(C) dependent
(D) breathable

2. People are not saddened or just _____ to live.

(A) engaging
(B) losing
(C) ruining
(D) struggling

3. Men have casual powwows with friends _____ tea.

(A) over
(B) under
(C) by
(D) to

4. Entertainment is hard to _____ in Niger.

(A) run over
(B) come by
(C) word for
(D) sign up

C *Based on the information in the passage, write "T" if it is true, or "F" if it is false.*

1. A dominant religion in Niger is Islam. (   )
2. People in Niger usually use silverware when they eat. (   )
3. Nigeriens like to have long arguments with foreigners. (   )

D *Rearrange the words and phrases in the (   ) to complete the sentences.*

1. 農家の人々は通気性のよい素材でできた穀物貯蔵庫に収穫物を保存する。
Farmers keep their harvest in (of / a / storage / materials / breathable / made / grain / structure).
Farmers keep their harvest in (____
____).

2. 私たちは、貧しい国の人は自分の生活に無力感を感じていると思いがちだ。
We often assume that (countries / people / in / helpless / feel / impoverished) about their lives.
We often assume that (____
____) about their lives.

Conversation

Listen to the conversation and answer the following. For ①, choose the right words. For ③, put the words in the { } in the right order. For ② and ④, fill in the blanks.

Kenta: I can't imagine what Nigerien food looks like. What kind of dishes are common in your country?

Cherifa: Well, I'd say we often have stewed dishes that are spicy.

Adamou: We eat *tuwo*, which is a loaf of pounded millet or corn, ① { coward is / co-worker's / covered with } a tomato stew or a thick okra sauce.

Kenta: What? Do you have okra in Niger? I wasn't expecting to hear that!

Cherifa: It's said that okra comes from Africa.

Kenta: I didn't know that. What else do you eat in Niger?

Adamou: We also eat rice. ② (   ) Japanese rice, it's dry though. But we also make pounded rice, which is like Japanese *mochi.*

Kenta: Really? It's quite surprising that you have *mochi* in Africa!

Cherifa: Hmm, what else... Yeah, we also ③ ({ *couscous* / occasions / for / eat / special } → ______________________________).

Kenta: *Couscous* is a tiny pasta that looks like rice, right?

Adamou: Right. And we also have skewered meat, which ④ (   ) (   ) to *yakitori*. We eat beef, mutton, chicken, and pigeon, too.

Kenta: Whoa! You eat pigeon! I wasn't expecting to hear that either!

Choose the picture that does not match the conversation and circle the number.

(1)

(2)

(3)

(4)

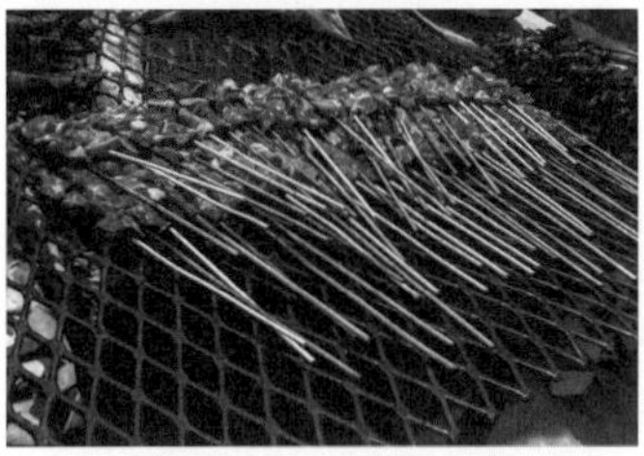

Column

文化を知るための Language：ハウサ語・ザルマ語等 (Hausa/Zarma etc.)

Gaiswa「ガイスワ」／Fofo「フォーフォー」

あいさつをするとき、話す相手が友人なのか、目上の人なのかなどによってあいさつの仕方が違ってきますよね。しかし、ニジェールではあいさつの仕方ではなく、あいさつに使う「言語」そのものを選ぶ必要があるのです。ニジェールでは、ハウサ語の「ガイスワ」やザルマ語の「フォーフォー」、フランス語の「サリュ」やアラビア語の「アッサラームアライクム」など、多言語のあいさつが飛び交っています。

多民族国家のニジェールでは、ハウサ族、ザルマ族、トゥアレグ族など、民族によって言語が異なります。「国語」とされる言語は 10 言語もあり、フランスの植民地であった背景から、公用語にはフランス語が用いられ、公的な場や中高等教育機関ではフランス語が使われます。また、イスラム教徒が多いニジェールでは、少しあらたまったあいさつにはアラビア語を使うなど、TPO に応じて使用言語の使い分けが自然に行われているそうです。

Group Presentation

1. Which do you prefer, (A) or (B)? Put a check mark (✓) and write your reason in the box.

☐ (A) In my free time, I prefer spending time alone.

☐ (B) In my free time, I prefer spending time with others.

Because ……………………………………………………………………………

……………………………………………………………………………………

2. Make a group with two or three partners who have the same preference and present your thoughts. Write down the important key words in each box while listening to others.

Key words: Group member 1	Key words: Group member 2	Key words: Group member 3

3. Using your group member's key words, form one collective opinion.

……………………………………………………………………………………

……………………………………………………………………………………

……………………………………………………………………………………

4. Present your group's opinion to the class.

Unit 14

Brazil: A Paradise for Soccer and Dance Lovers

サッカーとダンスが織りなす文化とは！

Pre-Reading Activity

Look at picture 2. Guess what the two men are doing. Talk to your partner in English.

Vocabulary Map

Use the words in the box to complete the vocabulary map.

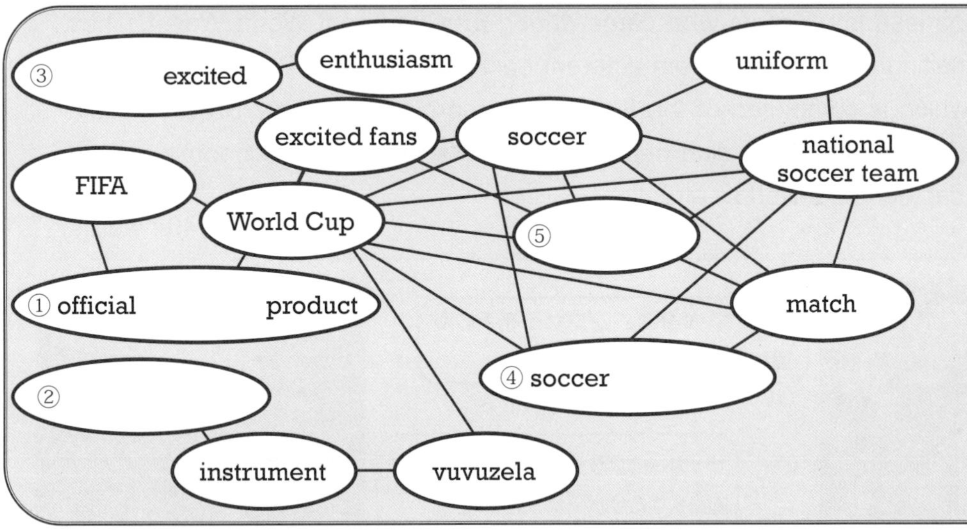

licensed
field
overly
percussion
cheering

Reading

41

When you imagine Brazil, many of you might think of soccer. Brazil has the most wins in the World Cup out of any other country. The Brazilian national soccer team is called "The Canaries" because of their vivid, yellow-colored uniform.

In 2012, a percussion instrument called the *caxirola* was created in Brazil. It was designed to be the official cheering instrument of the 2014 FIFA World Cup. The *caxirola* was widely advertised before the match and even became an official licensed product of FIFA. One of the reasons why they made it was they wanted to make something as popular as the vuvuzela, which was a commonly used instrument during the 2010 World Cup, held in South Africa.

The *caxirola* is a hand-size, round instrument that is filled with small particles. You shake it to make sounds. However, as soon as it was released, some overly excited fans threw their *caxirola* into the soccer field during the game. After that, their use was forbidden in multiple games, even before the World Cup started. Therefore, the *caxirola* didn't become the next vuvuzela due to the backlash caused by the Brazilian's enthusiasm for soccer, unfortunately.

The *caxirola* itself is based on the *caxixi* which is a traditional Brazilian instrument. It is a percussion instrument and consists of a closed basket with a flat bottom filled with seeds and other small particles. It makes sounds when it is shaken. It is often used during capoeira matches.

Capoeira is a Brazilian martial art that combines elements of dance, acrobatics and music. Although there are few official historical records, it is said to have been created nearly 500 years ago in Brazil by African slaves. Taken from their homes against their will and kept in slavery, they started inventing fighting techniques for self-defense. African slaves are also said to have created the samba dance. This dance is widely seen during Rio's Carnival. The Carnival is an annual festival that originally came from a Catholic event.

There are a lot of immigrants in Brazil from Africa, Europe, the Middle East, and 250,000 Japanese immigrants who came during pre- and post-World War II. Thus, Brazil is a melting pot of people from different backgrounds. Now Brazil is a member of BRICS, which is composed of the five major emerging countries: Brazil, Russia, India, China and South Africa. And because of Brazil's remarkable economic growth, it has been capturing the world's attention.

(404 words)

2010年W杯で、ブブゼラを手に応援をするサッカーファン

サッカーのブラジル国内戦で熱狂的に応援をするサポーターたち

Find the following words in a dictionary and write their meanings in the parentheses below. Fill in the bracket with an appropriate word to complete the phrase.

Words and Phrases			★ 予習しておこう！
out of any other ~	他のどの～よりも	enthusiasm	(　　　　　　)
canary	カナリア	consist [　　　] ~	～から成る
vivid	鮮やかな	martial art	武術、武道
percussion	振動、打楽器	combine	混ぜ合わせる
instrument	(　　　　　　)	acrobatics	アクロバット、曲芸
cheering	応援する	slave	(　　　　　　)
official licensed	公式に認定された	against one's will	自分の意志に反して
particle	(小さな) 粒状のもの	self-defense	護身、自己防衛
release	公になる、世に出る	Catholic	カトリック教会の
overly excited	(　　　　　　)	immigrant	移民
soccer field	サッカー場	melting pot	(人種・文化等の) るつぼ
forbid	(　　　　　　)	BRICS	ブリックス [新興工業国 5 か国]
multiple	複数の	be composed of ~	～で構成される
backlash	反感、反動	emerging country	新興国

Reading Exercises

A *You will hear three questions about the passage. Select the best answer and circle (A), (B) or (C).* 42

1. What makes Brazil a unique country?
   (A) There are many people with different backgrounds.
   (B) There are many traditional musical instruments.
   (C) There are many soccer fields designed for World Cups.

2.
   (A) They have
   (B) They have
   (C) They have

3.
   (A)
   (B)
   (C)

B *Circle the best choice to complete the following sentences.*

1. Brazil has the most wins in the World Cup _____ any other country.

(A) out of
(B) in front of
(C) instead of
(D) for

2. Their use was _____ in multiple games.

(A) forbid
(B) forbids
(C) forbidding
(D) forbidden

3. It _____ a closed basket with a flat bottom filled with small particles.

(A) consists of
(B) consisted of
(C) consisting with
(D) consisted with

4. African slaves were taken from their homes _____ their will.

(A) when
(B) against
(C) because
(D) under

C *Based on the information in the passage, write "T" if it is true, or "F" if it is false.*

1. The *caxirola* contains many small elements inside of it. (　　)
2. Capoeira is a kind of traditional dance that looks like fighting. (　　)
3. There were a lot of Japanese immigrants in Brazil. (　　)

D *Rearrange the words and phrases in the (　) to complete the sentences.*

1. 彼らのサッカー熱がもたらした逆効果のせいで、カシローラは第 2 のブブゼラにはならなかった。

The *caxirola* didn't become the next vuvuzela (enthusiasm / the backlash / by / due / their / to / caused) for soccer.

The *caxirola* didn't become the next vuvuzela (______________________________
______________________________) for soccer.

2. ブラジルは BRICS を構成する 5 つの主要新興国の一つです。

Brazil is a member of BRICS, (of / which / five / composed / the / is) major emerging countries.

Brazil is a member of BRICS, (______________________________
______________________________) major emerging countries.

Conversation

Listen to the conversation and answer the following. For ① and ④, fill in the blanks. For ②, choose the right words. For ③, put the words in the { } in the right order. 43

Kenta: I'm into acai bowls now. I make them for breakfast with lots of fruits and cereals.

Felipe: I heard acai bowls were popular in Hawaii first, but did you know the acai tree is ① (   ) from the Amazon region in Brazil?

Isabela: Acai is full of iron and calcium, and good for your health. It's called a super fruit.

Kenta: I had no idea! What other famous foods come from Brazil?

Felipe: Meat dishes. "Churrasco" is one of the most popular ones. The wait staff at churrasco restaurants ② { work a band with / walk around with / wall around his } skewers of meat and slice them onto the customer's plate. It's very entertaining!

Isabela: "Feijoada" is also a popular dish for Brazilians. It is said that the dish has its roots with African slaves.

Kenta: Oh, the stew with pork and black beans, right? I've seen it on TV, but ③ ({ bit / to / shocking / a / it / was } → ______________________________
______________________________) me.

Felipe: Was it? Then you might like *dobradinha*. *Dobradinha* is an intestine stew cooked with white beans, so the color is much lighter.

Isabela: We often eat feijoada on Wednesdays and Saturdays, and *dobradinha* on Tuesdays.

Kenta: Wow, that's interesting that some dishes are served ④ (   ) (   ) the day of the week!

Choose the picture that does not match the conversation and circle the number.

(1)

(2)

(3)

(4)

Column

文化を知るための Language：ポルトガル語（Português）

***café da manhã*「カフェ・ダ・マニャン」**

先住民の言語や移民が持ち込んだ言語など、100を超える言語が話されていると言われるブラジルですが、公用語はポルトガル語です。これはかつてブラジルがポルトガルの植民地であったためです。しかし、ヨーロッパにある国ポルトガルで話される言語とは異なる点が多々あるため、ブラジルで話される言語は「ブラジル・ポルトガル語」とあえて区別して呼ばれることもあります。

そんなブラジルでは、「朝食」のことを *café da manhã* と言います。これは文字通り訳すと「朝のコーヒー」ですが、コーヒーを飲まなくても「朝食」という意味で使えるそうです。コーヒーの輸出量が世界一のブラジルならではですね。

日本でも、「そろそろお茶にしよう」は「休憩しよう」という意味になりますが、必ずしもお茶を飲む必要はないという感覚と似ているかもしれません。身近な食べものは長い年月を経ると、その存在が当たり前となり、日常の言葉にいつの間にか定着していくことがわかります。

Group Presentation

1. Which do you prefer, (A) or (B)? Put a check mark (✓) and write your reason in the box.

☐ (A) I prefer watching sports at the stadium.

☐ (B) I prefer watching sports on the TV.

➡ Because ....

....

2. Make a group with two or three partners who have the same preference and present your thoughts. Write down the important key words in each box while listening to others.

Key words: Group member 1	Key words: Group member 2	Key words: Group member 3

3. Using your group member's key words, form one collective opinion.

....

....

....

4. Present your group's opinion to the class.

Unit 15

Sweden: Time for *Fika*

くつろぎのスウェーデン文化とは！

Pre-Reading Activity

Look at picture 1. Guess what it is. Talk to your partner in English.

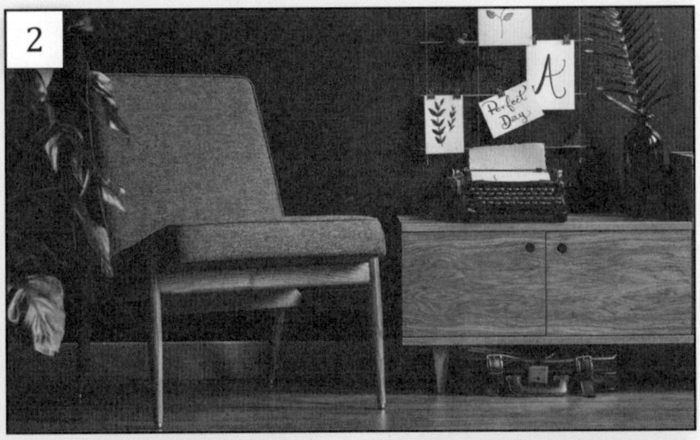

Vocabulary Map

Use the words in the box to complete the vocabulary map.

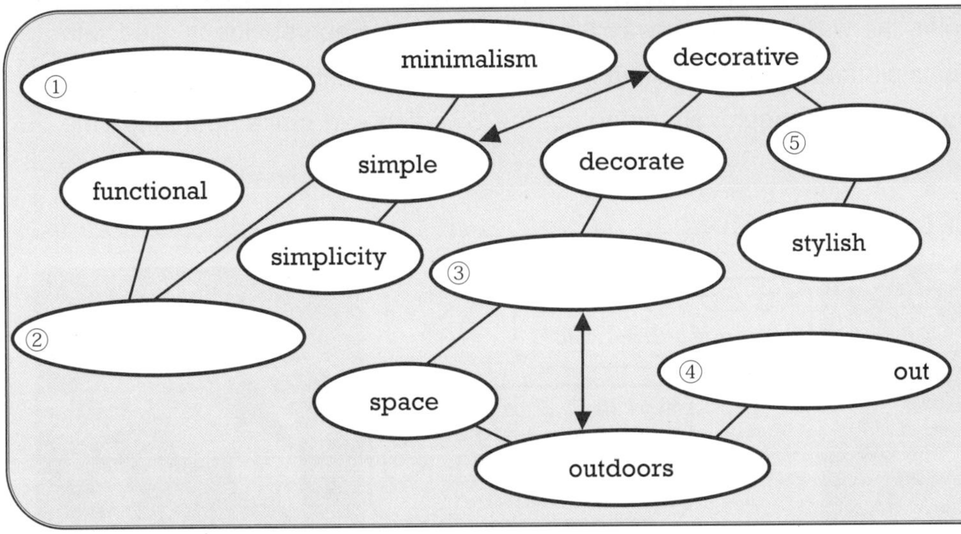

indoors

fancy

practical

functioniality

stay

Reading

44

When you think of Sweden, what things come to mind? You may think of the furniture shop, IKEA, or the fast-fashion clothes company, H&M. You may even think of the Nobel Prize. But have you ever heard of the Swedish ritual called *Fika*? *Fika* is a Swedish tradition of a coffee break that is more about socializing than drinking coffee. For the Swedish, *Fika* is about being comfortable and relaxing while enjoying all the good things in life. Some people take a short *Fika* and some take longer ones. It can be done alone or with a friend. Either way, the crucial factor for *Fika* is to take it easy.

To practice *Fika*, you need nice coffee or cake, as well as a comfortable space. The Swedish give importance to spending quality time relaxing indoors. This tradition could be related to the weather in Sweden. The summer is short, and the sun stays out until late at night. Some places have a phenomenon called White Nights, where the sun hardly goes down. However, the winter is fairly long and sometimes the sun goes down at around 3 p.m. Therefore, people tend to stay indoors and make their time as comfortable as possible. For example, they enjoy decorating a room with fancy furniture to help them relax.

Fika is such an important part of daily life. For example, at many Swedish offices, there is usually a *fika* break; once in the morning and again in the afternoon. Some people even bring a thermos of coffee and a baked good to have a *fika* while they are traveling. *Fika* is about taking time to slow down and enjoy the moment.

Swedish furniture is called Scandinavian design, and has features of simplicity, minimalism and functionality. They prefer practical design, but they also attach special importance to its distinctive style. That is why Swedish fabrics, furniture and knick-knacks are simple but stylish as well. In Sweden, design represents who you are, so people put a lot of effort into decorating their homes.

In Stockholm, the walls of the subway are one of a kind. Each station is filled with unique art on its platform walls or waiting hall. There are some stations that make you feel as if you are in a museum. By doing so, the Swedish can make spending time indoors more enjoyable.

(391 words)

家族とフィカを楽しむ
スウェーデンの子どもたち

世界中にファンがいる
スウェーデン人デザイナーの
スティグ・リンドベリ
デザインの食器

Find the following words in a dictionary and write their meanings in the parentheses below. Fill in the bracket with an appropriate word to complete the phrase.

Words and Phrases ★ 予習しておこう！

Nobel Prize	ノーベル賞	tend to ~	～する傾向がある
ritual	習慣的に行うこと	decorate	( )
socializing	社交	fancy	しゃれた
either way	どちらにしても	daily life	日常生活
crucial factor	重大な要素	baked good	焼き菓子
take it easy	気楽にやる	Scandinavian	スカンジナビアの
practice	（習慣的に）行う	simplicity	( )
as well as ~	～と同様に	minimalism	ミニマリズム
space	空間	functionality	機能性
give importance to ~	～を重要視する	practical	( )
quality time	充実した時間	attach	（～に重きを）置く
indoors	( )	fabric	生地
stay [ ]	（外に）出ている	knick-knack	（装飾的な）小物
phenomenon	現象	stylish	( )
White Night	白夜	represent	表す、示す

Reading Exercises

A *You will hear three questions about the passage. Select the best answer and circle (A), (B) or (C).* 45

1. What is special about *Fika*?
   (A) People go shopping at furniture shops in Sweden.
   (B) Nice coffee and food are enjoyed.
   (C) Traditional breakfast in Sweden was started there.

2.
   (A) Stations
   (B) Nights
   (C) People

3.
   (A)
   (B)
   (C)

B Circle the best choice to complete the following sentences.

1. *Fika* is a Swedish tradition of a coffee break that's more about socializing _____ drinking coffee.

(A) that
(B) which
(C) than
(D) as

2. The summer is short, and the sun _____ until late at night.

(A) goes down
(B) stays out
(C) never shows
(D) comes around

3. They enjoy _____ a room with fancy furniture to help them relax.

(A) decoration
(B) decorates
(C) decorating
(D) to decorate

4. People put a lot of _____ into decorating their homes.

(A) effort
(B) space
(C) relaxing
(D) simplicity

C Based on the information in the passage, write "T" if it is true, or "F" if it is false.

1. *Fika* should be done with a lot of friends. (　　)
2. In Sweden, it is allowed to have a *fika* break even at the office. (　　)
3. The Swedish try to decorate their homes as quickly as possible. (　　)

D Rearrange the words and phrases in the (　) to complete the sentences.

1. スウェーデン人は家でくつろぎながら充実した時間を過ごすことを大事にしている。

The Swedish (spending / to / importance / give / quality time) relaxing indoors.

The Swedish (____

______________________________) relaxing indoors.

2. 人々は家から出ないで、できる限り快適に過ごせる時間を持とうとする。

People (stay / to / tend / make / indoors / and) their time as comfortable as possible.

People (____

______________________________) their time as comfortable as possible.

Conversation

Listen to the conversation and answer the following. For ①, choose the right words. For ② and ④, fill in the blanks. For ③, put the words in the { } in the right order. 46

Kenta: What is a typical Swedish dish?

Robert: Meatballs, ① { I guess / I get / I go }.

Kenta: Really? Meatballs don't seem Swedish at all.

Emma: It's a popular Swedish dish. We eat them with lingonberry jam. It's a jam made from small, round, red berries.

Robert: You can ② (   ) "Swedish food" and see the images. You'll find plenty of photos of meatballs, and probably cinnamon rolls, too...

Kenta: Right. There's lots of meatball dishes with berry jam and potatoes. But what is the staple food in Sweden?

Emma: "Staple food" means a food that you eat the most and also eat regularly, right? The concept ③ ({ to / is / familiar / not / us / as } → ____________________ ____________________) in Western countries, as I have never heard those words until I came to Japan.

Kenta: Is that so?

Robert: Let me see..., the staple food in Sweden... Well, pasta might be it.

Emma: It can be potatoes, too.

Kenta: Really? I didn't know that potatoes could be a ④ (   ) (   )!!

Choose the picture that does not match the conversation and circle the number.

(1)

(2)

(3)

(4)

Column

文化を知るための Language：スウェーデン語 (Svenska)

***Lagom är bäst*「ラーゴム・エ・ベスト」**

スウェーデンには *Lagom är bäst*（ほどほどが一番）という表現があります。これはスウェーデン人の生活スタイルを表すのにぴったりの言い回しです。スウェーデン人は、全てのことにおいてほどほどであることが幸せへの鍵だと考えています。食べるのもほどほど、飲むのもほどほど、物を持つのもほどほど、趣味もほどほど、家事もほどほど、働くのもほどほどにするのがスウェーデン流です。

Lagom är bäst の *lagom* はスウェーデン人がよく使うことばで、日本語の「ちょうどいい」にあたります。*Lagom* は非常に便利なことばで、質問に対する返事としてもよく使われます。例えば、「調子はどう？」、「今日どんな天気？」、「この服どうかな？」などすべてに "*Lagom*" で返すことができます。スウェーデン人にとって *lagom* であることは、非常に重要なことです。スウェーデンには、頑張りすぎず、怠けすぎず、多すぎず、少なすぎず、ほどほどの心地よい生活ができる人が多いようです。

Group Presentation

1. Which do you prefer, (A) or (B)? Put a check mark (✓) and write your reason in the box.

☐ (A) I would spend more money on the interior decoration of my room than on my clothes.

☐ (B) I would spend more money on my clothes than on the interior decoration of my room.

Because ....

....

2. Make a group with two or three partners who have the same preference and present your thoughts. Write down the important key words in each box while listening to others.

Key words: Group member 1	Key words: Group member 2	Key words: Group member 3

3. Using your group member's key words, form one collective opinion.

....

....

....

4. Present your group's opinion to the class.

Guess What?! - Intercultural Surprises- [B-930]
Comprehensive Training for English "5" Skills: Read, Listen, Write, Speak, and Discuss!
世界の衝撃アイテムから学ぶ 15 の国の文化と人々
読んで聞いて書いて話して議論する！ 英語「5」技能総合訓練教材

第 1 刷　2021 年 4 月 1 日
第 4 刷　2024 年 3 月 29 日

著　者　松井　夏津紀　Natsuki Matsui
飯田　泰弘　Yasuhiro Iida
金田　直子　Naoko Kaneda
ケン・ウィング・プーン　Ken Wing Poon
ｱﾄﾞﾊﾞｲｻﾞｰ　横山　仁視　Hitoshi Yokoyama

発行者　南雲　一範　Kazunori Nagumo
発行所　株式会社　南雲堂
〒162-0801　東京都新宿区山吹町 361
NAN'UN-DO Publishing Co.,Ltd.
361 Yamabuki-cho, Shinjuku-ku, Tokyo 162-0801, Japan
振替口座：00160-0-46863
TEL：03-3268-2311（営業部：学校関係）
03-3268-2384（営業部：書店関係）
03-3268-2387（編集部）
FAX：03-3269-2486

編集者　田中　仁
製　版　堀田　華
装　丁　銀月堂
検　印　省略
コード　ISBN 978-4-523-17930-6　C0082

Printed in Japan

E-mail nanundo@post.email.ne.jp
URL https://www.nanun-do.co.jp